Boundless Theatre

presents

NATIVES

by Glenn Waldron

Natives received its UK premiere at
Southwark Playhouse, London, on 29 March 2017

NATIVES

by Glenn Waldron

Cast
A	Ella Purnell
B	Fionn Whitehead
C	Manish Gandhi

Director	Rob Drummer
Designer	Amelia Jane Hankin
Lighting Design	Zoe Spurr
Video Design	Cate Blanchard
Sound Design	Father
Movement	John Ross
Production Manager	Nick Slater
Stage Manager	Sarah Barnes
Assistant Stage Manager	David Putman
Costume Supervisor	Claire Wardroper
Set built by	SFL
AV Operator	Kostis Mousikos
Sound Engineer	Dominic Kennedy
Vocal Coach	Sarah Case

Costumes supported by	ASOS

Boundless Theatre wish to thank the following for their help with this production: Nick Carvell, Purple PR, Steve Alexander, Tim Waldron, Damaris Media, Mimi Farrer, Workspace, Old Vic Workrooms, Elliott Bornemann, Kike Brimah, Sam Angell, The Bush Theatre.

th— boundless boundl
boundless theatre th

THE COMPANY

Ella Purnell | A
Ella was recently seen starring in Tim Burton's feature *Miss Peregrine's Home for Peculiar Children* opposite Eva Green and Asa Butterfield.

She will soon be seen in the feature *Churchill* opposite Brian Cox and Miranda Richardson and the independent film *UFO* with Gillian Anderson.

Ella's film debut was in Mark Romanek's *Never Let Me Go* playing the young Keira Knightley, she went on to play the young Angelina Jolie in *Maleficent,* starred opposite Clive Owen in *Intruders*, and also featured opposite Aaron Taylor Johnson and Chloë Grace Moretz in *Kick Ass 2.*

She was one of Screen International Stars of Tomorrow 2010.

Fionn Whitehead | B
Fionn will next be seen as the lead role in Christopher Nolan's feature *Dunkirk* opposite Mark Rylance, Tom Hardy and Kenneth Branagh and has just finished shooting the young lead in *The Children Act* opposite Emma Thompson and Stanley Tucci directed by Richard Eyre. Fionn made his screen debut playing the title role in the critically acclaimed, three-part drama *Him* for ITV1 and was named one of Screen International Stars of Tomorrow 2016.

Manish Gandhi | C
Manish trained at LAMDA on a full scholarship. He was included in the British Council's 2016 Global list of 33 cultural influencers from around the world promoting freedom and equality.

Theatre includes: *Now We Are Here* (Young Vic); *Brown Shakespeare* (Efua Theodora Sutherland Drama Studio, Legon-Accra); *Rizwan* (FTII Pune); *Limbo* (Prithvi Theatre Mumbai); *Cock* (Prithvi Theatre/National Centre of Performing Arts, Mumbai).

Film includes: *That Transient Interval* (Whistling Woods International); *Chai Shai Biscuits* (Picture Thoughts) and *Rizwaan* (FTII Pune).

Television includes: *Rides upon the Storm* (DR/ARTE); *Judwa Raja* (Disney); *Na Bole Tum* (Viacom 18).

Radio includes: *A Meeting by the River* (The Animals Podcast).

Glenn Waldron | Writer

Glenn Waldron is a London-based playwright and writer. A former magazine editor and journalist, Glenn was Editor of *i-D* magazine and his feature writing has appeared in the *New York Times*, the *Guardian*, the *Independent*, *Vogue*, *W* magazine, and other publications. His first play *Forever House* premiered at the Drum, Theatre Royal Plymouth and his work has since been performed in Germany, Norway, the Netherlands and the USA. Upcoming productions include *The Here and This and Now* at TRP and *End of the Pier* at Hackney Showroom. Glenn also lectures in journalism and pop culture at the University of the Arts London.

Rob Drummer | Director

Rob Drummer joined Boundless Theatre in July 2016 as Artistic Director. He previously worked as co-director on the company's production of *Sense* by Anja Hilling at the Academy of Live and Recorded Arts (ALRA), alongside Andrea Ferran. He was a mentor to emerging playwrights from the UK, Germany, Netherlands and Norway on the European Writers' Lab component of the company's Theatre Café Festival. Prior to becoming Artistic Director of Boundless Theatre he was Associate Dramaturg at the Bush Theatre where he ran the Literary Department, responsible for all playwriting work including the commissioning and development of new plays for production. He has established ongoing partnerships with Playwrights of New York (PoNY), delivered projects with Kudos Film & Television and established a partnership with Drama Centre London and Oberon Books on the Student Guide to Writing: Playwriting. Before joining the Bush Drummer was the first Literary Manager for HighTide Festival Theatre where he supported the expansion of the festival, doubling the number of productions, and for HighTide he also directed *Eisteddfod*, *Endless Poem* and *Perish*. As a dramaturg and director he has worked with playwrights at theatres including the National Theatre, Hampstead Theatre, Bristol Old Vic, Contact, York Theatre Royal and Theatre503. He was one of the first recipients of an Artists' International Development Fund from the Arts Council and British Council and spent time working in South Africa with playwrights and theatre makers at the Baxter and Market Theatres.

Amelia Jane Hankin | Designer

Amelia trained at RADA and the RSC.

Recent design credits include: *good dog* (Watford Palace Theatre); *The Same Deep Water As Me*, *The Crucible*, *Pinter Triple Bill*, *Dealer's Choice* (Guildhall); *Rudolf* (West Yorkshire Playhouse); *Torch* (Edinburgh Festival); *We Are You* (Young Vic); *Bricks and Pieces* (RADA/Latitude); *The Neighbourhood Project* (Bush); *This is Art* (Shakespeare in Shoreditch); *The Tiger's Bones* (Polka/West Yorkshire Playhouse); *The Little Prince* (Arcola); *Night Before Christmas* (West Yorkshire Playhouse); *She Called Me Mother* (Tara Arts/national tour); *Fake It 'Til You Make It* with Bryony Kimmings and Tim Grayburn (national tour/Traverse/Soho) and *64 Squares* with Rhum and Clay (national tour/Edinburgh Festival).

Amelia's designs for The Itinerant Music Hall were exhibited at the V&A Museum as part of the MAKE/BELIEVE UK Design for Performance exhibition July–January 2016.

Zoe Spurr | Lighting Design

Zoe trained at the Royal Central School of Speech and Drama. Recent theatre lighting designs include *School Play* (Southwark Playhouse); *good dog* (Watford Palace/UK tour); *The Truth* (Central Szinhaz, Budapest); *Muted* (The Bunker); *Erwartung/Twice Through The Heart* with Shadwell Opera (Hackney Showroom); *The Knife of Dawn* (Sackler Studio, Roundhouse); *Affection* and *Hookup* with Outbox Theatre Company (Hackney Showroom/Contact Manchester/Site Specific); *Torch*, *This Evil Thing* (Edinburgh Fringe Festival 2016); *A Serious Case of The F*ckits*, *The Heresy of Love* (Central) and *Bitches* (NYT/Finborough). Corporate designs include the Terry Pratchett Final Book Launch at Waterstones Piccadilly Circus, and *Grey Goose Fly Beyond* at the Welsh Presbyterian Chapel, Shaftesbury Avenue.

Cate Blanchard | Video Design

Cate Blanchard studied Theatre Practice at the Royal Central School of Speech and Drama where she now works as a visiting lecturer in Video Design for Performance. Cate has previously worked at Apple for five years teaching Mac-based programs. As a practitioner, Cate enjoys devising situations and as a designer has worked with ranging companies across the UK. Favourite shows include: *Why the Whales Came* (UK tour/Wizard Presents/LAMDA rep season; directed by Philip Wilson); *Amphibians* (Offstage Theatre; directed by Cressida Brown; OffWestEnd Award); *The Magic Flute* (English Touring Opera UK tour); *The Changeling* (Southwark Playhouse). Cate is currently working on devised collaboration with the Royal Central School of Speech and Drama and Complicite.

Father | Sound Design

Joe Farley and Freddie Webb are the duo behind Father, a music composition and sound design studio. Using a variety of approaches that bridge musicality and sound design, they create provocative and emotive sonic landscapes which look to create a truly immersive experience. Their work spans film, documentary, commercials and live performance – *Natives* is their first theatre production.

John Ross | Movement

Trained: London Contemporary Dance School.

As a performer he has collaborated with companies and choreographers including the Royal Opera House, Jorge Cresis, Freddie Opoku-Addiade, Ace Dance & Music, Two Thirds Sky, SmallPetitKlein, C12 Dance Theatre, Opera North, Tom Dale and Jasmin Vardimon.

Recent work as movement director includes: *Faust* (Vilnius City Opera); *Treasure Island* (Birmingham Rep); *Deny, Deny, Deny* (Park); *Labyrinth*, *Deposit* (Hampstead); *Henry V* (Regent's Park Open Air Theatre); *Talent*, *Diana of Dobson's* (New Vic); *Jumpy* (Clwyd Theatr Cymru); *Treasure* (Finborough); *One Arm* (Southwark Playhouse). Choreography for John Ross Dance includes: *Blink, Wolfpack* (Tour/V&A's Theatre and Performance Archive); *Man Down* (UK tour/international tour); *Little Sheep*, alongside commissions for Dance United, Shoreditch Youth Dance, DanceEast, Scottish School of Contemporary Dance and Old Vic New Voices.

Awards include: Donald Dewar Award (2010), New Adventures Choreographer Award (2013), and MOKO Children's Choreography Award (2014).

In 2015 he was named as one of the BBC Performing Arts Fund's 32 Ones to Watch.

Nick Slater | Production Manager

Nick has worked as a freelance production and technical stage manager since 2013. His recent projects include: *Grounded* (Gate); *Rotterdam* (Trafalgar Studios); *World Factory* (Metis); *Ross & Rachel* (Motor); *Shh!* (C-12 Dance) and *Early Days (of a better nation)* (Coney). Other projects include *The Cocktail Party* (Print Rooms); *Electric*, *Knife Edge* (Big House). Prior to 2013 Nick worked at the Young Vic Theatre and led projects within their Taking Part department. These included *The Sound of Yellow* (Matthew Xia), *The Beauty Project* (Kirsty Housley), *The Surplus* (Jonathon O'Boyle), *All Stones, All Sides* (Finn Beams) and *Now Is the Time To Say Nothing* (Caroline Williams).

Sarah Case | Vocal Coach
Sarah Case is a highly skilled and experienced voice and
text coach. She was Head of Voice on the Acting Degree at
Italia Conti Academy for fourteen years and is now Head
of Voice for Fourth Monkey Actor Training Company. She
co-directed *Tamburlaine the Great Parts 1 & 2* for Fourth
Monkey at Jackson's Lane theatre. She also teaches
students and teachers at Shakespeare's Globe Education.
As a creative voice director, Sarah has worked on many
shows including *Richard III*, *Macbeth*, *The Winter's Tale*,
Widows, *Our Town*, *Machinal*, *Phaedra's Love*, *and Way to
Heaven*. She has taken numerous professional workshops
including Physical Voice in the Moving Body (Patricia
Bardi), Lamentation with Marya Lowry, and many more. She
holds a Postgraduate Diploma in Voice Studies from
Central School of Speech and Drama, a BA (Hons) in Drama
from Manchester University, and a postgraduate acting
diploma from Mountview. Sarah is author of *The Integrated
Voice* (Nick Hern Books 2013).

WE ARE BOUNDLESS THEATRE

Boundless Theatre creates exhilarating, relevant and shareable theatre with and for young people and curious others. Our work responds to a vibrant and diverse global culture. We empower, inspire and invest in future audiences and artists now and promote conversation and exchange across the UK, Europe and internationally.

'They shake up expectations of what "theatre for young people" is or could be' (A Younger Theatre, 2015)

Boundless Theatre (formerly Company of Angels) was founded in 2001 by John Retallack, to foster and produce new and experimental theatre for young audiences. The company continues to push the boundaries of theatre for young audiences through award-winning work across the UK and internationally. Its productions have won critical acclaim and have been nominated for numerous awards (Stage Award, TMA Award, Herald Angel Award, Time Out Critics' Choice). Through its flagship Theatre Café Festival it has presented translations of over 90 of the best new plays for young audiences, collaborating with artists, audiences and arts organisations from 22 countries.

'Smart, mischievous and genuinely thought-provoking' (*Financial Times* on *World Factory*, 2015)

For 10 years we have led provision for early career artists, nurturing their talent through dialogue and exchange with other cultures, artforms and young people, resourcing risk-taking and supporting work through to production. We have achieved huge success in empowering Associates to become visionary, confident and exceptional artists (alumni includes Associate Director at the Old Vic, Artistic Director of the Gate Theatre, Associate Director, International at the Royal Court).

'The experience has been life changing, not only for the children, but for the staff involved too' (Headteacher)

Beyond its productions and artist development, Boundless Theatre delivers a range of projects with schools and universities across the UK. We inspire, challenge and empower young people by connecting them to exceptional artists, European influences, nurturing their creativity and fostering ownership of our work.

www.boundlesstheatre.org.uk

boundlessabound

BOUNDLESS TEAM

Artistic Director (Joint CEO)   **Rob Drummer**
Executive Producer (Joint CEO)   **Zoë Lally**
Associate Producer   **Phoebe Ferris-Rotman**
Administrator   **Atiha Gupta-Armstrong**
Finance Manager   **Mark Sands**

BOUNDLESS BOARD

Charles Granville (Chair)
Charlotte March
Jake Orr
Carolyn Unstead

BOUNDLESS ADVISERS

We want to make relevant work that enables 15 to 25-year-olds to see theatre as a vital part of their cultural experience. To keep us in check and to ensure we are being provoked to be ambitious with our plans we have an Advisory Group made up of seven brilliant young people who are drawn from different backgrounds: from theatre to parkour.

Our Advisers meet with us regularly to see plays, talk big ideas, attend events and discuss what excites them most about being young today.

Robert Awosusi
Max Baraki
Adrian Gardner
Angela Legg
Maya McFarlane
Finlay Ross Russell
Ashley Scantlebury

Photograph © Christian Sinibaldi

BOUNDLESS SUPPORT

Philanthropic support from individuals and Trusts & Foundations is vital to the future of Boundless Theatre. Your support helps us to empower young people across the UK, create theatre of the highest standard for 15-25s and nurture the best new artists to respond to this audience. We just can't do it without you.

To discuss ways of supporting Boundless Theatre please contact Zoë Lally, Executive Producer at **zoe@boundlesstheatre.org.uk**

BOUNDLESS ENTHUSIASTS

For those of you that believe as we do that every young person deserves the opportunity to be inspired by the highest quality theatre, we welcome your enthusiasm and support! The most valuable way of receiving support is through regular monthly donations. This means we can plan ahead and take more risks with our work, finding new ways to engage and empower young audiences, participants and artists.

To make a donation please visit **www.justgiving.com/boundless-theatre**

BOUNDLESS FUNDERS

We are currently supported by Arts Council England as a National Portfolio Organisation. Our International Theatre Club project is funded by the European Union (Erasmus +).

We are grateful to the following organisations for their previous support:

Anglo-Swedish Literary Foundation
Austrian Cultural Forum
Awards for All
Bourne Trust
Children's Forum Ltd
City of Quebec
Coutts & Co
Clore Duffield Foundation
D'Oyly Carte Charitable Trust
Ernest Cook Trust
Esmee Fairbairn Foundation
Education
Audiovisual & Culture
Executive Agency
EU Creative Europe
Cultural Commission
EU Culture 2000 Programme
Foyle Foundation

Goethe-Institut
Help a London Child
Hillingdon Community Trust
Lloyds TSB Foundation
Mercers Company
Moose Foundation
Nederlands Instituut
Network for Social Change
Paul Hamlyn Foundation
Peter Minet Trust
Pro Helvetia
Redhill Trust
Romanian Cultural Institute
Royal Netherlands Embassy
Southwark Theatres Education Partnership
Swedish Embassy and Wates Foundation

Boundless Theatre is a registered charity no. 1089185

THE ORIGIN OF THE TEENAGER
Jon Savage

During 1944, Americans started to use the word
'teenager' to describe the place of youth in their
society. From the very beginning, it was a marketing
term that recognised the spending power of adolescents.
Within a culture that thought of business in terms of
national identity and individual freedom, the fact that
youth had become a market also meant that it had become
a discrete, separate age group with its own peer-
generated rituals, rights and demands.

The coining of the word 'teenager' marked the
emancipation of adolescence. It also resolved a deep-
seated problem within America and Northern Europe. Youth
had been seen both as an enigma and a threat ever since
the dawn of civilisation, but the political, economic
and cultural upheavals of the late eighteenth century
gave the discussion of its status a new urgency. It was
during this period that the romantic idea of youth as a
separate, stormy, rebellious stage of life began.

Within the instability created by the beginnings of the
mass society, the revolutionary nature of youth
threatened to have dire consequences. These were played
out during the next one hundred years, with anarchist
uprisings and an upsurge in juvenile delinquency. By the
last quarter of the nineteenth century, the whole nature
of Western society was coming under review: as the clash
of empires loomed, youth was charged with a new
importance. It appeared to offer the key to the future.
Would it be dream or nightmare?

Between 1875 and 1945, there were many attempts to
envisage and define the status of youth within the mass
age. Many adults, concerned about what they saw as a
savage, wild stage of life, made concerted efforts to
regiment adolescents through national policies. Others
tried to capture and redefine the potential of youth, in
artistic and prophetic visions that reflected the wish
of the young to live life on their own terms. These were
the beginnings of what became known in the early 1940s
as youth culture.

Within all these definitions, there was a distinction
between biological and cultural age. Puberty had long
been recognised as a physical state, but those
undergoing its rigours were routinely called 'children'
well into the twentieth century. In the same way, adults
in their twenties and thirties actively participated in
the youth culture of the 1910s and 1920s, and were still
thought to be young. Until the invention of the teenager

in 1944, most discussions of youth offered fluid definitions of both age and name.

The first person to propose a coherent redefinition of puberty was the American psychologist G. Stanley Hall. In 1898, he proposed that the life stage that he called 'adolescence' should cover the years between fifteen and twenty-four. Although the first definitions of the Teenager in 1944 were aimed at seventeen-year-olds – who were then the most visible consumers – the age range would expand upwards after the Second World War. When the term became an international buzzword during the mid-1950s, it enshrined Hall's original definition.

America's victory in the Second World War created the empire that still holds sway in the twenty-first century. The invention of the Teenager coincided with this victory, and indeed the definition of youth as a consumer offered a new ideal within a devastated Europe. For the last sixty years, it has dominated the way that the West sees the young, and has been successfully exported around the world. Like the new world order that it heralded, it is in need of some redefinition.

This is an extract from *Teenage: The Creation of Youth Culture 1874-1945*, by Jon Savage, published by Pimlico.

'Southwark Playhouse churn out arresting productions at a rate of knots' *Time Out*

Southwark Playhouse is all about telling stories and inspiring the next generation of storytellers and theatre makers. It aims to facilitate the work of new and emerging theatre practitioners from early in their creative lives to the start of their professional careers.

Through our schools work we aim to introduce local people at a young age to the possibilities of great drama and the benefits of using theatre skills to facilitate learning. Each year we engage with over 5,000 school pupils through free schools performances and long-term in school curriculum support.

Through our participation programmes we aim to work with all members of our local community in a wide ranging array of creative drama projects that aim to promote cohesion, build confidence and encourage a lifelong appreciation of theatre.

Our theatre programme aims to facilitate and showcase the work of some of the UK's best up and coming talent with a focus on reinterpreting classic plays and contemporary plays of note. Our two atmospheric theatre spaces enable us to offer theatre artists and companies the opportunity to present their first fully realised productions. Over the past 24 years we have produced and presented early productions by many aspiring theatre practitioners many of whom are now enjoying flourishing careers.

'A brand as quirky as it is classy' *The Stage*

For more information about our forthcoming season and to book tickets visit www.southwarkplayhouse.co.uk. You can also support us online by joining our Facebook and Twitter pages.

NATIVES

Glenn Waldron

Acknowledgements

Rob Drummer, Phoebe Ferris-Rotman, Zoë Lally and all at Boundless Theatre, Teresa Ariosto, mentors and friends from Company of Angels' European Writers' Lab including Jorieke Abbing, Kristofer Blindheim Grønskag, Elisabeth Coltof, Michel Decar, Paulien Geerlings, Tale Naess, Jakob Nolte, Lot Vekemans, Henrik Adler, Øystein Ulsberg Brager, Lutz Huebner and Sarah Nemitz for your continued support, Stefan Fischer-Fels and all at Düsseldorfer Schauspielhaus, Jan Friedrich, Jessica Hoffmann and all at Hartmann & Stauffacher, Virginia Leaver, Megan Vaughan, the Bush Theatre, Amy Dolamore, Sophie Wu, Tom Ross Williams, James Cooney, Jessica Sian, Kike Brimah, Elliott Bornemann, Sam Angell, and everyone who participated in *Natives* workshops, Tom Oldham, Alex and Ellie at Kate Morley PR, Dan Jones, Tim Waldron and all at Damaris Media, Harriet Pennington-Legh and Becca Kinder at Troika, Sam Smith.

G.W.

A German-language version of *Natives* was first performed at Düsseldorfer Schauspielhaus in September 2016.

'We must approach the idea of "digital natives" with caution…
One of the hardest yet most important things we as a society
must think about in the face of technological change is what has
really changed – and what has not.'

danah boyd

'Each new generation is a fresh invasion of savages.'

Hervey Allen

'Fuck those skinny bitches,
fuck those skinny bitches in the club…'

Nicki Minaj

Characters

a.
b.
c.

All aged fourteen

Note on Play

The lines at the beginning of the play can be divided up between a., b. and c.

a. b. and c.

The Great God Creton had three hundred daughters and sons by three hundred different wives but the most favoured of all his children was the youngest.

The Child was the offspring of Creton and Lanthea, a wild, free-spirited huntress, and just like her mother, the Child possessed a natural curiosity and fearlessness.

Whilst Creton's other daughters and sons spent their days training to be great warriors and wise counsellors and renowned thinkers, the Child was free to roam the breadth of Creton's kingdom, each day returning home at sunset with a new discovery for her delighted father and mother; a giant moth frozen solid as it emerged from its chrysalis; the first blue blossom of spring.

It was on a day in late summer that the Child found herself on the edge of the Valley of Thorns. Here was the one place in Creton's entire kingdom that was forbidden to her but, being naturally curious, she did not see the harm in exploring.

Soon upon entering the valley, however, she realised why her father had not wanted her to see this place. For she had supposed all the subjects of her father's kingdom to be as free and happy as she was. But as she entered the valley, she suddenly found herself in a shadowy place full of misery and desperation. A place where the men, women and children of other captured tribes worked day and night as slaves.

And the sight filled her with a sadness that she could not shake.

The following day, the Child found herself summoned to the Great Hall to read for her father, but as soon as she entered, Creton could see the sadness on the Child's face and, at once, the Great God's countenance suddenly changed. 'You have visited the Valley of Thorns!' he declared angrily.

The Child tried to deny it but at this, the Great God Creton flew into an almighty rage that shook the heavens and rent huge rifts across the earth for ten thousand nights.

'I love you with all my being,' explained Creton to the Child. 'But you have disobeyed me and have saddened me to the very depths of my spirit. In punishment, I will give you a new name and a new nature. And you will go to live with the wise people of Aros.' The Child pleaded desperately with her father, for Aros was forty days and nights away by boat, but the Great God in his anger would not be swayed and the following morning Creton tearfully watched as the ship carrying his favourite child set sail for Aros.

It was twenty nights into the journey when a mighty storm swept across the ocean, tossing the boat high into the air before splitting it violently in two.

When the Child awoke the following morning, she found herself entirely alone, washed up on the shore of a small, rocky island. She set about exploring her new dwelling place but soon found it to be a dark, barren spot with little of any note, save for some caves around the shoreline and the wild sheep that roamed its stony outcrops.

Blessed with her mother's resourcefulness, she spent the day spearing fish, gathering firewood and setting traps for the sheep, before promptly falling asleep as soon as she had made a fire.

It was pitch black when she later awoke and, with a growing sense of terror, saw a series of creatures slowly and silently emerge from the caves along the shoreline. What kind of animal they were, the Child could not say, for the ragged beasts were covered in filth and mange and uttered sounds that she could not understand.

And thus several years passed on the island; the days filled with hunting and fishing and the nights with the watching of the ragged beasts until, slowly but surely, the Child forgot about her old life, so that when one morning a boat appeared at the shoreline, she did not at first recognise the man emerging from it. Recognise him as her own father. Only when she ran down to greet Creton at the water's edge did the memories of her past life return, and the Child wept openly just like her father did – for Creton himself had searched for many years to find her.

It was only when Creton pulled the Child towards him in a fierce embrace that she caught sight of her own reflection in the water and was shocked to see that her time on the island had transformed her appearance beyond all measure – looking back at the Child in the reflection was not the daughter of a Great God but the image of one of the wild, ragged beasts that she had been so fearful of.

Creton, unaware of the Child's revelation, drew her ever closer to him. 'My beloved child, my beloved child, you must never ever leave me again,' he declared with a great fury. 'Please, swear it now.'

But on hearing this, the Child suddenly drew away from her father (for she did not understand that the anger Creton expressed was an anger towards himself).

'What?' Creton asked. 'What is it, Youth?' (For this was the new name that Creton had given the Child in her disobedience.)

And a mighty rage suddenly filled Youth's heart.

And she thought of all the things she would say to her father.

How it was her father's actions that had reduced her to such a lowly state.

How she did not deserve to be abandoned this way.

How it was her father and his forefathers who had already failed, not her.

How she understood so much more than he could imagine.

How she would gather together all the ragged beasts, all the other wild ragged beasts of the island and together they'd set sail for somewhere new, together they'd find a new world of their own making.

And Youth summoned up all the strength in her body but, to her great dismay, found that she could not speak.

For she no longer remembered the many words of her father's tongue. And, hard as she tried, only two words would come out of her mouth.

Two words that she had never uttered before.

Two words dropping to the ground like dull, muddy stones.

Two words to begin a war.

The words flash up, one after the other.

Fuck.

You.

Perhaps they then flash together. Music. Some kind of visual introduction to a., b. *and* c.

a. *doing her make-up perhaps,* b. *pumping iron, etc. Then:*

a.   It's the morning of Lily Kwok's Funky Fourteenth Birthday Dance and I'm sat in Miu Miu.

I'm looking at things on my phone while I wait for Amber.

I'm sat on the pistachio-green velvet banquette you always sit on in Miu Miu, taking small sips of the Lime Cucumber Juleps they always give you in Miu Miu.

And – and I live on a small, clean island with a twenty-per-cent tax ceiling and eighty-four-per-cent humidity, floating somewhere in the Indian Ocean.

b.   I'm looking at things on my phone and this guy's giving me evils.

He's really giving me evils!

a.   I'm looking at things on my phone and also counting.

Counting the seconds between sips of the Lime Cucumber Julep.

Because there's a perfect number.

Because Suki Newhouse read in *Vogue* that the optimal ingestion rate for liquids is exactly one sip per thirteen seconds and that's the perfect number.

c.   Fourteen.

It's the day of your fourteenth birthday and you have a test.

Your fourteenth birthday.

A test!

a.   And I'm counting the sips but also looking at the feed on my phone.

I'm going through all the pictures and videos everyone has posted in the last forty-six seconds.

Everyone at the Orchard Hills All-Girls Academy for Academic Excellence.

(That's my school.)

And I'm looking at this picture Bettina Rice-Peters has posted and I really can't decide.

I'm really, like, not sure.

Whether it's worth five hearts or six.

It's this close-up of a Smoky Egyptian Cat's-Eye she's tried for Lily Kwok's Funky Fourteenth Birthday Dance and it's not a seven. It's definitely not a seven!

It's a little scrappy around the waterline and the line should, like, kick out at the end not just swoop and it's definitely not a seven.

And Annika Albrecht did a Smoky Egyptian Cat's-Eye last week with a perfect kick.

And she had an aggregate score of five-point-nine.

So how can this be a six?!

c.   It's the day of your fourteenth birthday and you have a test.

Your fourteenth birthday.

A test!

And you're still in bed and it's your fourteenth birthday and the test and – and the one thought follows the other.

The first thought about the birthday and then the second thought about the test and the two combined make you think it's not fair.

It really isn't!

And then you wish that something would happen to your school.

Just for a second but –

That something has happened to your school overnight.

Something – really bad.

Bad enough that all today's tests are cancelled.

Like, maybe there's been this, this super-galactic storm and a giant meteor-ball of fire has landed on the school.

Or maybe it's been invaded by slugs!

By the giant evil slugs from the *Legend of Porto*!

Giant evil slugs who have crawled up from the sewers, covered the school and started, like, *devouring* it.

And it's only for a second.

And you don't mean something like bad-bad.

You don't mean, like, bombs or –

And you know that you can't make this happen, the wishing couldn't make it happen.

But still, you think, what if it's happened?

What if something bad-bad's happened overnight?

Because it could have.

It really could!

And you take it back.

And you say it out loud.

Just in case anyone's listening.

Just in case the Almighty happens to be listening.

'I take it back.'

'I take it back.'

a. I take it back and give her six hearts.

Because the swoop is actually quite kicky.

And Jennifer Cheng Khoo's given her four.

Which is so, like, harsh.

Just really – *harsh*.

And then I'm, like, scrolling through my feed and I'm looking at a video that Mia Ferrero has just shared.

This video of her fact-finding trip to the West Bank last weekend for history class.

And even though I'm fundamentally in favour of Mia's proposed two-state solution, unlike Christy Vanderbilt and Jennifer Cheng Khoo who are, like, so *Zionist* in outlook, I think the film is essentially a little reductive in its argument and I give it seven hearts.

And then I'm looking at this video that Summer Klatten-Smith has posted of her new pug. And I'm giving it a full nine hearts (minus one for respiratory issues) when I get a message from Brooke.

Brooke who's also waiting for Amber.

Brooke who has two hundred and thirty-six more followers than me and three hundred and seventy-eight more followers than Amber and also once held a python in *Teen Vogue*.

Brooke who thinks Amber is Literally Taking Forever.

That's what the text from Brooke says: 'Amber is Literally Taking Forever.'

Five exclamation marks four smiley faces one kiss.

And I text back straight away.

'God, I know.'

'Tell me about it, babes.'

Three eye-rolls two egg timers one kiss.

And then there's a bleep and I check my phone but it's not mine.

It's actually Brooke's.

Brooke who is… sat there right next to me on the pistachio-green velvet banquette in Miu Miu.

Brooke who checks her phone and smiles. Or smiles as much as Brooke does.

And then the store's sending over a sales representative with more Lime Cucumber Juleps.

And she's asking us all these questions.

Questions about Lily Kwok's Funky Fourteenth Birthday Dance (because, like, everyone on this island knows about Lily Kwok's Funky Fourteenth Birthday Dance).

And as we answer the questions, she's nodding and laughing.

Even though what we're saying isn't necessarily – funny?

And then she's asking Brooke 'What's your favourite song to dance to?'

And at this, Brooke and I just burst out laughing.

Which is not a particularly cool thing to do in the face of the sales representative in Miu Miu.

But we can't help it, the bursting-out laughing, we really can't!

Because – no one actually dances at Lily Kwok's Funky Fourteenth Birthday Dance.

No one would ever dance at Lily Kwok's Funky Fourteenth Birthday Dance.

That just isn't a thing that could – happen.

And the idea of it is just crazy.

It's crazy!

b.   I'm watching this thing on my phone and the old guy opposite me's giving me evils.

He's one of these Harry Potter-headmaster types and he's giving me real evils.

And – and I'm looking at him like, alright, chill.

What's your problem, dude? Relax.

No biggie, mate.

No one's died.

And I mean, technically that's not true.

Technically we're at a funeral and – and technically he's the vicar.

But, y'know, not really a problem, is it?

Not really hurting anyone, is it?

And because, what am I meant to do?

Listen to old Dumbledore bang on about the Gospel of the Good Samaritan?

You're alright.

You're good.

c.   Your good trousers are still dirty from the day before.

Still dirty from when Big Mohammed gave you a wedgie in lunch break – and then accidentally dropped you in the dirt.

And now you can't find any clean trousers to put on.

And your room's a mess, your room's always a mess.

And you finally find some trousers but the trousers belong to Ali.

Your older brother Ali who you share a room with.

And even though it's the only clean trousers you can find.

And even though he borrows your things all the time.

You know that if he catches you wearing them, then he'll go mad.

Like, completely mental.

And then he'll probably give you a wedgie too.

And why is everyone always giving you wedgies?

b.   He's giving me evils, old Dumbledore, and then they're doing some hymn.

Some really boring, crappy hymn.

Something about *ploughing the seed and scattering*.

I mean, What The Actual, yeah?

And I put my earphones in and go back to what I'm watching.

The thing I'm watching on my phone.

It's this film about this Japanese gangster.

He's a Japanese gangster but he also happens to be a cannibal.

But then one day, he, like, decides to be good, yeah?

And instead of just killing Japanese men for money, he decides to rescue all these women.

All these super-fit Japanese women.

Only sometimes, on account of his innate cannibalistic nature, the temptation's too much and he accidentally eats them.

He accidentally eats all the super-fit Japanese women.

It's sick, man.

It's really sick!

c.   It's not that funny.

It's really not!

You're in the main room of the house and everyone's there having breakfast.

Your father and your sisters.

Everyone except your older brother Ali.

And because you can't find any trousers, then you've come to breakfast in your pants.

Only the pants you're wearing – the pants you're wearing are not really your best pants.

They're the ones your Auntie Fatemeh bought you when you were nine or ten.

Your blue superhero underpants with the red and yellow 'S' on them.

And maybe it's funny – the blue pants with the 'S' on them – maybe it's a bit funny.

But it's not *that* funny.

It's not!

And your father and mother are laughing.

And all your sisters are trying to smack you on your bottom and, like, pinch your cheeks (the cheeks on your face).

And your face is going redder and redder when – when you see this package on the table.

This small flat package wrapped in coloured paper.

And – and you know it won't be what you hope it is.

You know it's really not what you hope it is.

But, still, your heart is, like, jumping in your chest.

And you make a deal.

A deal with the Almighty.

If the small flat package wrapped in coloured paper is
a copy of *Hiro's Kingdom 5* then you'll make your bed
for a year.

Or – or six months.

Definitely for a month.

If it's *Hiro's Kingdom 5*, you'll definitely make your bed.

Definitely for a week.

a.   (*Takes earphones out.*) Approximately, like, nine years,
     seven days and forty-two hours after entering the Miu Miu
     changing room, here's Amber.

Amber finally reappears.

Comes out in this burnt-ochre crêpe de Chine blouse with
pussybow detailing.

I'm sitting on the pistachio-green banquette with Brooke
and Ariana.

And Amber's standing in front of us saying 'What do you
think?

What do you think of the burnt-ochre crêpe de Chine
blouse with pussybow detailing?

And of course, we already know about crêpe de Chine
blouses with pussybow detailing.

Know that they are everything.

Literally Everything.

Know this because of Leonora-Rose Sandford.

Know this because three days, five hours and forty-seven minutes ago, she arrived late to Wellness & Centering wearing one.

Marched through the classroom to her desk with Elena Carvelo and Aisha Premji, wearing one like she was modelling for Gucci.

Which, FYI, she's done – she's literally done.

And now we're in Miu Miu and Amber's saying 'What do you think?'

What do you think of her burnt-ochre crêpe de Chine blouse with pussybow detailing.

And – I don't know.

I'm really not sure.

Because this crêpe de Chine blouse is different enough to the crêpe de Chine blouse I'm wearing to Lily Kwok's Funky Fourteenth Birthday Dance.

And to Brooke's crêpe de Chine blouse (which is actually not crêpe de Chine anyway, it's more of a *crêpe charmeuse*).

But then I'm looking at Brooke and I know what Brooke's thinking.

That maybe burnt-ochre is too close to the burnished copper of her Gucci crêpe de Chine blouse.

Also that there's a possible clash with my winter metallics contouring.

Also that Coco Chanel once said that 'Beauty begins the moment you decide to be yourself' and, frankly, she's not sure if Amber is really a burnt-ochre kind of person.

And by this point, she's looking worried.

By this point, Amber's looking kind of desperate.

Because we've already been to Prada, Escada, Topshop, Dior, Gucci, Pucci, Céline and Alexander Wang and none of them have crêpe de Chine blouses with pussybow detailing in Amber's size.

And there is no possible way that Amber can go to Lily Kwok's Funky Fourteenth Birthday Dance without some kind of variation on a crêpe de Chine blouse with pussybow detailing.

And there is no possible way that Amber can not-attend Lily Kwok's Funky Fourteenth Birthday Dance and still go to our school.

No possible way that she can not-attend Lily Kwok's Funky Fourteenth Birthday Dance and – basically still live.

And me and Ariana both look to Brooke.

Brooke who is sitting there in her oversized Gucci aviators.

And then Brooke says the Miu Miu crêpe de Chine blouse with pussybow detailing is nice.

It's 'nice'.

But the way Brooke says it, the way Brooke says it's nice, twitching her nose like some expensive cat, Amber knows.

She totally knows.

c.   It's not *Hiro's Kingdom 5*.

It's not even *Hiro's Kingdom 4* or *3*.

Or – or *Legend of Porto*.

It's just a book!

This really old, dusty book.

And your father's saying how it's full of wisdom.

And how you'll read it and then become wise.

And all this stuff about how it will make you a man, how you'll read this and you'll finally stop being a little boy and become a man.

And then one of your sisters says 'But Baby Pumpkin already thinks he's Superman' and then they all start laughing at you again.

And then your father is laughing too.

And maybe because you're getting a bit annoyed.

Maybe because you're getting a bit annoyed or maybe because it's your fourteenth birthday and all you've been given is a dusty old book, then you turn and ask him.

Turn to your father and ask him this question.

This really bad question.

Ask him if your brother has read the book and is that how he became a man?

Ask him if your brother's now the man of the family because he's the one that pays for all the food?

And what does Ali do anyway?

What exactly does Ali do?

And where does he go at night?

Where does Ali –

And – and your father reaches across the table and hits you across the cheek.

Hard.

And – and then no one's laughing.

No one at the table is laughing at all.

b.   Georgia Smith is total Fit As!

I'm at this funeral in this nothing-church in this nothing-town in this nothing-country and now we're doing this hymn.

This really crappy boring hymn.

And Georgia Smith is sat right behind me.

Georgia Smith!

Georgia Smith who's in actual fact my cousin but only, like, a second cousin.

So, like, totally game on!

And I catch her eye and Georgia's giving me this look.

This, like, really sad look.

And it's the first time Georgia Smith's ever noticed me.

First time since she got Fit As.

So I look at her and do the sad look back.

Like this:

Perhaps a. *and* c. *do it.*

And she's looking at me with her best sad look.

And I'm looking back at her with my best sad look.

Like this:

Again.

And then she's doing this smile, this really sad smile.

Like this:

Once again.

And that's when I do it.

That's when I lean in.

Lean in and whisper 'Wouldn't mind ploughing and scattering my seed with you sweetheart yeah?'

Do it until she stops.

Stops doing the sad smile and just looks down instead.

Not got proper tits yet anyway.

Beat.

c.   *Hiro's Kingdom 5!*

    Hiro's Kingdom 5!

It's there beside your bed when you go back in your room.

There but you never noticed it in all the mess.

And beside it, a note from your brother, Ali.

Your brother Ali who is now officially your favourite family member.

Officially your favourite person ever.

'Happy Birthday' it says and then the name he calls you.

And you don't know the English word for the name he calls you but it basically means 'sheep's anus'.

And you don't know where Ali got the money from, you don't know where Ali gets all of his money from but right now you really don't care because – *Hiro's Kingdom 5*!

And your fingers are like itching. They're literally itching to start playing.

But you stop yourself and for a moment, you just sit there.

You sit there and wait.

Sit there and enjoy the moment.

The anticipation.

Hiro's Kingdom 5!

Sit there for so long that your mother shouts that you're going to be late for school and you realise that now you'll have to wait.

Wait until you get back from school.

Nooooo!

b.   Slaggy Amy and Fat Jess.

Slaggy Amy and Fat Jess!

I'm looking around the church and that's the only people here from school.

Slaggy Amy and Fat Jess!

And Slaggy Amy's bawling her eyes out.

Probably cos she always fancied him and now she'll never get to give him one.

And her eyes have, like, run all down her face.

Like some big slaggy panda!

And then Fat Jess is just sitting there in her big black puffa.

Just staring straight ahead.

And I'm looking round the church.

And no one's really here.

No Eggs or Richie. Mikey. Little Andrew.

I'm looking around the church and no one's here.

None of the lads.

And that's cool.

That's – totally cool.

a. *and* c. *look at* b.

Like – whatever.

I put my earphones in and go back to what I'm watching.

c.   And then – and then you're leaving for school.

You've had your breakfast.

Washed your bits.

Dressed.

Packed your bag.

Finally found some trousers.

And as you leave, your mother says all this stuff.

All this stuff she always says when you leave the house.

Even now.

Even now it's safe.

'Speak to no one.'

'No one's business is your business.'

And most of all: 'Don't make trouble.'

And as usual when she says this, you laugh.

You do this laugh because, a) your mother says this every time you leave the house.

And b) you've never started a fight in your whole life.

You really haven't!

And anyway, the city is safe now.

This part of the city you live in, it's – safe now.

And the fighting – the fighting is somewhere else.

And the last few years feel like a dream.

And there's no sound of gunfire in the distance.

No getting lost because a street is suddenly not there.

No burnt bodies in the gutter.

And as you walk through the streets to school, you see other people.

Men hurrying to work.

Children going to their nursery holding hands.

And everywhere, people painting.

Painting their houses and building new ones where the old ones used to be.

Moving into new ones.

And sometimes you wonder where they went.

The family who lived in the apartment next to yours.

The old man at the corner who sold the cigarettes.

The people –

The people who have gone.

But – it's good now.

Everything here is good now.

That's what your brother says.

That everything is good.

Everything here is good.

a.   I'm sitting on the pistachio-green banquette with Brooke
and Ariana.

And Ariana's just posted a picture.

A picture of us all drinking the Lime Cucumber Juleps
they always give you in Miu Miu with the caption: 'Julep
time, bitches… so much fun!!'

And I'm hearting the picture when I get the message from
Brooke.

The message about Amber.

Brooke telling me that there's no space in the car tonight
for Amber.

No space in the car for Amber and how I have to, like,
tell her.

And at first, I don't really understand what Brooke's saying.

Because – because we were just in Brooke's car.

And there was obviously plenty of room for Amber in the
car because Amber's really small and the car's actually
very big.

And also, Amber was just, like, in it.

And then I look over at Brooke.

Brooke who is barely visible behind her oversized Gucci
aviators.

And suddenly I do.

Suddenly I get it.

And I look round the store and over by the handbags, there's these two women.

These two bored-looking women with, like, really polished skin.

And they're looking at this handbag, this silver-chained cross-body in textured panther, and I can see in the way they're talking that they must be related.

That one of them must be the mother and one of them the daughter.

But I really can't tell who is who.

I can't tell which is which.

b.   The vicar's giving me evils again.

They're doing a prayer or something and I'm watching the Japanese Gangster Cannibal thing and it's getting to a really good bit and Georgia Smith is a frigid no-tits bitch and old Dumbledore's giving me evils again.

He's really, like, giving me evils.

And now he's actually pissing me off.

He's really actually starting to really piss me off.

Because it's not like he can hear it, the vicar dude.

Not like he can hear the thing I'm watching on my phone.

Not like he can really hear it.

Not – until we all kneel for the prayer and the earphones come out the socket.

Blast the whole church with, like, gunfire.

Oops!

But at least he's just started shooting people.

The Japanese Gangster.

Least he's not started, like, torturing them yet.

Or, like, *eating* them.

a. *and* c. *look at him.*

b.   What?

c.   Yasin has just farted!

It's the second lesson of the day and it's history.

And everyone is looking in Yasin's direction because he's just done this really big, wet-sounding fart.

Like – (*Makes the sound of the fart.*)

And you don't want to smell it, you really don't want to smell it but then – argh! – you also don't want to be left out.

Also a fart is actually just a combination of nitrogen, hydrogen, carbon dioxide, methane and oxygen, so how bad can it be?

And you don't want to smell it. But then you sort of do.

Just to see how bad it is.

And so you do.

You sort of sniff and –

It's nothing.

It's nothing really.

It's not a good smell but it's not that bad, it's nothing like the sound but then –

Oh!

Oh my life.

It hits you.

Oh!

A wave of the nastiest, dirtiest, most toxic smell you have ever smelt.

Ever.

It is off the scale!

Like, if you made a chart of all the bad smells in the world, then you'd need extra paper and some tape to show where it is on the chart.

Oh!

Like the smell of a rotting sheep carcass mixed with your grandfather's bad breath and then, and then a bag of seven-day-old rubbish. All rolled into one… and then made worse!

It is so bad that it is actually quite incredible.

Incredible that someone has made this, that the insides of someone's body has made this smell.

And everyone's kind of going crazy and like coughing, and like looking at each other, and pretending to gasp for air.

But then the teacher's ignoring it and it's beginning to disperse.

And the teacher's talking about the Glorious History of this Country.

Of this city.

And the teacher's saying all this stuff and –

And some of it makes sense and that's good but then –

Some of it doesn't – hang together.

There's bits missing.

There's definitely bits missing.

And he's saying how lucky you are, lucky *we* are to be on the good side.

How lucky we were to fight off the rebels. The terrorists.

And everyone's writing it down.

They're all writing that down.

And then you're wondering if everyone thinks they're on the good side.

If everyone everywhere thinks that too.

If anyone ever thinks they're on the bad side.

And, like, maybe some people *are* on the good side.

Like Hiro. Like Hiro in *Hiro's Kingdom*.

But maybe sometimes they're just on the side that wins.

Maybe sometimes it's not the good side but just the side that wins.

And how the people in the city, the people in the other city called your city the rebels.

Called you the terrorists.

And then you're thinking about this family.

And even though they are a Western family and, like, a cartoon family, they are just like your family.

They really are!

And you think how the cartoon family don't go to prayers or eat the food you eat or even speak the language you speak but how the cartoon family are sort of like your family too.

And you think, which side are the yellow family on? Which side are the yellow cartoon family on?

And that's what you're thinking when the teacher asks if anyone has any questions.

Which side are the cartoon family actually on?

You don't ask the teacher that though.

Of course you don't ask the teacher that though.

b.   And then the prayer's over and they're playing this song, this really crappy song,

This song they only play to, like, make people cry.

And they're playing this song and he didn't even like it –

He really didn't like it.

Thought it was just a bit – shit.

And then – and then they take the flowers off the box and.

The box is moving.

It's actually moving.

And I'm looking at this travelator and I'm looking at this shiny wooden box as it moves slowly forward.

And I've still got my earphones in and my brain's trying to connect.

Thinking what it looks like.

And I'm watching this wooden box and it's moving along this thing, this conveyor belt and I realise what it is.

What it looks like.

A checkout. The checkout at Tescos!

It really does!

And the box is moving and –

And I'm thinking how it's just like the checkout at Tescos and.

And how you could, y'know like, put some beers and frozen pizzas on it.

If you wanted.

Put some beers and frozen pizzas on it alongside the wooden box that's slowly moving.

And the thought of that.

The thought of that sort of makes me – laugh.

And I mean, not really planning to.

Not really intending to but I sort of do.

I laugh.

Because it's funny.

Or sort of funny.

And I think maybe he would too.

Find it funny.

I really do!

Maybe if he wasn't –

Maybe if it wasn't –

Maybe if it wasn't my brother's body in the box – then he would find it funny too.

Beat. Everyone looks at him.

What?

Pause.

a.   And then – and then we're done in Miu Miu so we head to Balenciaga.

And we're in Balenciaga and I'm sat with Brooke on the caramel velvet banquette and we're sipping triple-chilled Lychee Coolers.

And Amber's in the changing rooms trying on more crêpe de Chine blouses with pussybow detailing.

And again, I'm counting my sips.

And I'm doing this online lesson in Advanced Mandarin for Business just for fun.

Also because the Massachusetts Institute of Technology is increasingly looking for applicants who are at least trilingual and with a firm grasp of shifting Sino-American geopolitics and that's my parents' preferred tertiary education destination.

And I'm alternating this with the live feed of a speech on Ethics and Corporate Responsibility from an international finance summit in Berlin.

And I give the speech eight hearts.

Partly because the woman speaking makes some valuable points regarding the important role of philanthropy in today's shifting economic landscape.

And partly because the woman in the video is my mother and –

I miss her.

Beat.

b.   And then the funeral's over and I'm back in my room.

And everyone's down the pub.

Mum's already down the pub.

And I've done my crunches and my reps, had a toastie.

And I'm in my room and I'm thinking about the church.

How none of the lads were in the church.

And fair enough, funerals are pretty gay, yeah, but, like, could have made the effort.

Eggs and Richie, Mikey, Little Andrew.

Not like they're especially busy, yeah? Not like they're got *prior engagements*, yeah?

I mean – whatever, yeah.

It's totally –

And now I'm just on the phone.

Looking at things.

A quizzical look from a. *and* c.

Just y'know… 'Stuff'.

(*Embarrassed.*) What?

And I'm on my phone looking at stuff and Eggs, my best mate Eggs, has sent me this video.

We always send each other videos.

Things we like.

Things we're in to.

Have pretty much the same taste so…

But this video he's sent me is really strange.

S'weirding me out.

c.   The video's good but not that good.

It's break now and you're with your friends.

And you're watching this Drake video, the new Drake video on your friend's phone.

And it's not as good as the old Drake video but it's still Drake and it's still good and.

And then your friend says 'Look at this.'

And you all look at this video.

This other video.

This video of a man being thrown off a roof.

This man who is probably a homosexual or, being thrown off a roof.

And it's in your city, the video's in your city.

And you recognise the place and you maybe recognise the person.

And they're nothing new.

These videos are nothing new.

And they're kind of secret. They're not online these videos and you don't know where they come from.

Just something that gets sent round.

And all the people in them are unclean and they're nothing new. That's what your brother says.

That the people in them are all unclean and they're on the bad side and.

And that's why everything's better now.

That's why the city's clean again.

That's why it's safe.

And the man you sort of recognise is wearing this blue scarf.

He's on the edge of the building wearing a blue scarf.

And two official men are holding him.

Two official men with their faces covered are holding him.

Holding him over the edge of the –

And then one of them adjusts the scarf.

Lifts the scarf and adjusts the scarf and ties it.

Ties it around the man the other man's eyes and you realise the scarf is not just a scarf.

It's a blindfold.

And all your friends are laughing and cheering as the man is held over the edge.

They're all laughing and cheering and saying all these things and then –

And then –

And then one man pushes the other man off the top of the roof and –

And then they're not.

Beat.

And then your friend shows you the trailer for this new film.

This new one you've been waiting for for ages.

It's all your favourite superheroes come together.

All except Batman and Superman and –

And it's cool.

It looks so cool!

And you watch through it and it's just amazing.

And then you realise that you're late.

All of you are late for the test and you have to run.

b.   I'm running through them in my head.

I'm looking at the video Eggs has sent me and I'm running through them in my head.

All the reasons he might have sent it me.

Because – it's alright. It's definitely alright.

But nothing special.

Nothing extraordinary.

Not our usual thing.

Just – standard.

And the woman in it, the girl in the clip – the same.

Face, a six.

Body, at best, a five.

Standard.

a. *and* c. *look at him.*

And I don't really get it. I don't really get why he's bothered sending it.

Because it's definitely alright but nothing special.

Face, a six.

Body, at best a five.

But then – but then I see his message and he's like 'Bet Miss Jeffries will cheer you up, mate.'

And I watch it again and – ohmygod it's true!

She does!

She looks just like Miss Jeffries!

From Geography!

Perhaps an image of Miss Jeffries.

She really does!

The woman or. Girl or –

Or a bit like, anyway. Enough.

Got the glasses and – and it's funny.

Funny because Miss Jeffries is so, like, uptight.

Can't really imagine her doing –

Can't really imagine her with, like, one guy.

Never mind three.

Can't really imagine Miss Jeffries being – yeah.

Reaction from a. *and* c.

And I'm looking at the video, the video of Miss Jeffries-who-is-not-Miss-Jeffries and it's funny.

It's funny but it's also – naughty, yeah!

And suddenly, I'm getting –

Getting a little bit –

Hard.

c.   It's hard but not that hard.

The test.

It's sums and equations and you're always good at those.

And you like it because there's always an answer.

There's always a right answer.

It's never – confusing.

Never 'Oh but what about this?'

It's clear and definite.

Yes or no.

Right or wrong.

Clean. Precise.

And that feels good.

That feels – right.

And you've completed all the answers and you've finished early.

And now your mind's beginning to wander.

And you're thinking about *Hiro's Kingdom 5*.

And you're wondering if Hiro's shield still has the power to stop time.

And you're wondering if the princess is still trapped in a block of ice at the top of Old Drathusa's Mountain, just waiting to be melted.

Waiting there on the edge.

And then you're thinking about the man and you're wondering what it feels like.

Wondering what it feels like to fall.

Wondering whether you have time to think.

Wondering whether you actually have time to – feel.

And then good sides and bad sides.

And good people and bad people.

And there's something about the video.

Something about the blindfold or –

And – it's nothing to do with you.

It's got nothing to do with you at all.

And it's your birthday.

It's your fourteenth birthday!

a.   And we're sat in Balenciaga waiting for Amber.

And I'm looking at the new Drake video on my phone and it's not as good as the old Drake video but it's still Drake and it's still good and.

And then I spot that someone has commented on the picture Ariana has posted.

The picture of me, Brooke and Ariana on the pistachio velvet banquette in Miu Miu.

And the comment is Jess Wu saying how much she loves my lip colour.

And I heart the comment because Jess Wu's father is the head of Coutts and is also super-nice.

And then underneath it, Florence Adenuga has added another comment,

'Is that a beauty spot above your lip? So gorgeous, exclamation mark' and seven people have hearted it and I heart that as well.

And then below that, Iris Cargill-Durst has written this comment.

Iris Cargill-Durst who I barely know, I really don't!

Below it, Iris Cargill-Durst has written 'Is that a beauty spot or a wart?'

And – it's nothing.

It's only Iris Cargill-Durst and no one's hearted it.

And it's fine and it's nothing and it's only Iris Cargill-Durst.

But I'm so busy looking at the comment that I temporarily forget to count my sips.

And I put the glass of triple-chilled Lychee Cooler to my mouth and I sort of inhale and gasp.

I sort of inhale and gasp both at the same time.

And a small jet of triple-chilled Lychee Cooler explodes from my nose and mouth.

b.   (*Gobs a load of green gunk at* a.) Pah!

a.   A small jet of triple-chilled Lychee Cooler explodes from my nose and mouth on to my Alexander Wang.

c.   (*Gobs a load of green gunk at a*.) Pah!

a.   I'm sat next to Brooke on the caramel velvet banquette and triple-chilled Lychee Cooler has literally just erupted from my nose and mouth.

b. *and* c. Pah!

a.   And for a moment, I'm sort of, I'm sort of frozen.

And I can feel this redness creeping down my head.

From the top of my skull down to my face and neck.

And I'm dabbing at the triple-chilled Lychee Cooler speckling my Alexander Wang T-shirt and I'm thinking how Brooke has obviously seen it.

Has obviously just seen the triple-chilled Lychee Cooler speckling my Alexander Wang.

But then I look over at Brooke.

Brooke who has not in fact noticed the volcanic eruption of triple-chilled Lychee Cooler from my mouth because she's busy liking a video of our classmate Chiara Lachmann riding a horse in a trilby.

And I'm so relieved that Brooke is busy liking the video of Chiara Lachmann that it's kind of a surprise when my own phone vibrates and it's a message from Ariana.

Ariana who is sat the other side of Brooke.

'Enjoying your drink, sweetie?' she says.

all.   Four exclamation marks. Three cocktail emojis. Three surprised faces. No kiss.

a.   And – it's fine.

It's really nothing.

It's fine.

I mean, it's quite funny really.

When you – think about it.

And I get up from the caramel velvet banquette and I tell Brooke I am going to the restroom.

And Brooke maybe nods or maybe doesn't.

And then I slowly walk to the restroom.

And I dab my T-shirt down.

And then I'm looking in the mirror at this mark, this tiny mark above my top lip. And it's nothing really. Not even a skin tag.

It's not a beauty spot or a wart.

It's just a – blemish. Just this tiny, tiny blemish.

And it's fine. It's really fine.

And it's only Iris Cargill-Durst.

And Iris Cargill-Durst only has two hundred and nineteen followers and her pictures rarely get an aggregate score above a low seven.

And her nose is slightly crooked if you look at it in natural daylight.

And it's just this tiny blemish. This really tiny blemish.

And it's fine, it's really fine. And it's not like anyone has actually hearted it.

Iris Cargill-Durst's comment.

Not like Elena Carvelo or Aisha Premji have hearted it.

Not like Leonora-Rose Sanford has actually seen it.

And I stand in the centre of the restroom and I listen to the violin music they're piping into it.

And I wonder where the music is coming from.

I wonder where the music is coming from and I wonder how they found a caramel-coloured sink the exact same colour as the caramel-coloured banquette.

And then I wonder which came first the caramel-coloured sink or the caramel-coloured banquette.

And then I'm looking in the mirror and suddenly I see that Ariana is standing in the doorway.

Ariana is standing in the doorway looking down at something on the floor by my feet.

And it's then –

It's only then that I look down and realise I've pressed the nails of one hand so hard into the palm of the other that it's broken through the skin and begun to bleed.

And blood is dripping down the sink.

Dripping down the sink and pooling on the caramel-coloured floor.

Beat.

The other two stop what they are doing and look at a.

a. *doesn't know what to do.*

Only a little bit.

It's not –

No one knows how to proceed.

b.   And I'm in my room and I'm looking at this video of Miss Jeffries.

And I'm trying to – finish off.

But my – my thing it's not really *working*.

I mean it normally does. It definitely really does but –

And then the doorbell goes.

The doorbell goes and I head downstairs.

I sort of – adjust – and I head downstairs.

And I can see through the wobbly glass, it's Fat Jess.

Can see because she's wearing this, like, massive puffa.

Can see because it's taking up all the glass.

Fat Jess in all her puffered glory.

And as I open the door, she does this look, this really sad look and I can't see another sad look so I go all cocky.

Like 'What, who died?'

And she tries to smile at this, she really tries to smile at this.

But it's not funny at all.

And the trying-to, the trying-to look on her face makes me feel –

Makes me feel, just –

And to cover it, I'm all like 'Alright Fat Jess.'

Even though I know it's kind of nasty.

Even though calling Fat Jess Fat Jess is quite a nasty thing to say.

But Fat Jess isn't bothered.

She's actually not fazed at all.

And Fat Jess is like 'Wanna go somewhere?'

And I'm like 'Spose.'

And then we shut the door and go.

a.   When I come out the restroom, Amber's stood there.

Stood there in front of Brooke and Ariana in this blouse.

A Balenciaga crêpe de Chine blouse with pussybow detailing in tarnished pink.

And Amber's saying 'What do you think?'

And we're both not-looking at Brooke but we're both waiting for her to speak.

And Amber's saying again. 'What do you think?'

And eventually.

Ten years, fourteen days and thirty-seven minutes later, Brooke speaks.

all. 'It's – nice.'

a.   It's nice.

And this nice. This nice is different to the other nice.

This nice is actually a good nice.

Or – nice enough.

A six-hearts kind of nice.

And I can tell Amber's relieved.

Think she might be quietly, like, *crying* or.

Only a bit but.

And then Brooke's telling Amber how she needs to, just, relax.

How she really needs to have more fun with fashion.

And Amber's nodding her head seriously and saying she will.

She totally promises that she'll have more fun with fashion.

She, like, totally will.

And while we wait for Amber to pay, I check my phone and – six people have hearted Iris Cargill-Durst's comment.

Six.

And it's fine.

It's really – fine.

And it's not like it's Aisha Premji.

Not like it's Leonora-Rose Sanford.

It's no one.

And it's fine.

It really is!

b. We walk down the road and head down to the Marshes because that's the only place to go.

We don't speak or anything but that's okay with me.

And the not-speaking is actually quite nice.

And she's doing that walk that all the girls round here do.

Arms crossed.

Marching straight ahead.

Like she's really pissed off.

And I want to ask her why all the girls round here do that.

But I know I probably shouldn't.

And we go past the pub, past the old swimming pool.

Past the new estate they never finished.

And we go to this place where – it's hard to describe but it's deep in the wood bit.

A bit where no one ever bothers you.

Not even the meth-heads or the gypos.

A wooded clearing.

A bit where it's quiet.

And Fat Jess takes off her puffa.

Fat Jess takes off her puffa and puts it on the ground for us to sit on, which is actually a really nice thing to do.

And as we sit there, I look at Fat Jess.

And I have this revelation.

That Fat Jess is not particularly fat at all.

It was just her big black puffa.

Fat Jess is actually not fat at all!

a.   After Balenciaga, we go to André's.

It's the most exclusive café on the island and we get the best table because Brooke knows the maître d'.

And Brooke orders a Virgin Mary with no ice because *Harper's Bazaar* said you consume three point four per cent less calories by drinking liquids at room temperature.

And then Amber orders a Virgin Mary with no ice.

And then Ariana orders one as well and –

And then I order one too.

And I check my phone and – and now twenty-two people have hearted Iris Cargill-Durst's comment.

And underneath it, a new comment from Suki Newhouse:

'Wonder if it's infectious?'

And underneath that, Iris Cargill-Durst has posted a picture of the Wicked Witch of the West, with this great big wart on her chin and the word 'Warthog' written across it.

And already seventeen people have hearted it.

And now I'm wearing this McQueen shirt.

I've changed into this McQueen shirt with a Peter Pan collar and –

And the Peter Pan collar is, like, digging into my neck.

And why is there no air-conditioning in André's?

And why can't I breathe?

And then a small chocolate cupcake with a small pink candle arrives at the table.

And suddenly everyone's looking in my direction.

And for a moment, I'm wondering whose birthday it is.

For a second, I'm wondering whose birthday it is and why is everyone suddenly looking at me?

And the Peter Pan collar is getting tighter and –

And that's when I realise why everyone's looking at me.

Because it's my birthday.

My fourteenth birthday.

Only we don't ever celebrate it.

Because –

Because you can't exactly have your birthday on the same day as Lily Kwok's Funky Fourteenth Birthday Dance, can you?

b. *and* c. *stop what they're doing.*

I'm mean you can't though, can you?

c.   You try to make the afternoon speed up but you can't.

You really can't.

It's the afternoon and you're stuck in school but you're desperate to be back home playing *Hiro's Kingdom 5.*

And then the lessons finally end and you're running home.

And as you run home, you pretend that you're Hiro in that scene from *Hiro's Kingdom 2.*

The one where he's underwater but suddenly he's got fins and flippers and it's like he's moving through air!

And you pretend that the people in the street are the giant sea snakes.

And you, like, duck and dodge around them and secretly shoot lasers out your eyes at them.

And you're running through the streets, dodging round people and instantly, like, vaporising them.

But then you're thinking about the video.

The man in the video.

And you're sure it's the brother, the brother of this kid you know.

Amir.

This kid called Amir, and the brother's name was – Zia.

And Amir is the same age as you and his brother is two years older.

Which makes Zia sixteen.

Made Zia sixteen.

It makes the man thrown off the roof sixteen.

And you remember Zia was always on a skateboard.

Would go skating with your brother Ali.

Always on this skateboard and always listening to Drake.

And as you pass the park, you remember this time when he was on a skateboard and you were in the park and he skated past you.

Him and Ali skated past you.

And Ali skated past you and called you a name.

And you don't know the English word for it but it basically means 'the testicles of an old horse'.

And then Zia skated past you.

And the way Zia skated past you, skated past you and landed in this awesome kickflip, it reminded you of your favourite character from the cartoon yellow family.

And for some reason – for some reason, you suddenly shouted after him, 'Don't have a cow, man!'

And you don't know why you said it.

And you thought he would, like, maybe turn around and call you a little freak or – or maybe beat you up.

But then Zia, then the boy called Zia turned around.

Turned round, looked at you and laughed.

Laughed like this was the funniest, most brilliant thing
someone had ever said.

And you thought that was cool.

Because he was an older boy, you thought that was a pretty
cool thing to do.

And you're passing the park and you're running through
the streets and you're Hiro in *Hiro's Kingdom 2* and
you're underwater and –

The boy called Zia and the blindfold.

The blindford that's actually a scarf and –

And you barely knew him.

You didn't really know him.

And it's nothing to do with you.

And you're nearly home.

You're very nearly home!

b.   Fat Jess has hit me!

Suddenly Fat Jess says this word and hits me.

Like, punches me on the arm.

Hard!

And then, like, runs away.

And I'm like going What-The-Actual, literally What-The-
Actual –

Before I remember it's this game.

This thing we used to play as kids.

When we were, like, six or seven.

And then we're running around.

And Fat Jess is running from me and I'm, like, trying to catch her.

And then she's running round and trying to chase me.

And we're screaming and we're whooping and –

And it's really dumb, the whole thing's completely dumb but it's also kind of – fun.

Sort of – nice.

a.   They're not nice at all.

Lukewarm Virgin Marys are not nice at all!

And we're sat there with the chocolate cupcake in André's and we each have a fork.

And we take it in turns to have a mouthful of the cupcake.

But really we're not eating it.

Really we're just reducing it to crumbs.

And we're sitting there in silence pretending to eat this cupcake.

And I'm looking at Brooke and Amber and Ariana.

And, for some reason, I'm thinking about this time.

When we were all six.

Four or five or six.

When me, Brooke, Amber and Ariana were in the bath together.

And Amber told us if you poo in the bath then it turns into chocolate milkshake.

We used to share baths together!

And then because Brooke had, like, this insane laugh and because I always wanted to hear it so badly then right there and then, I did it.

I did this massive poo.

Right there in the bath!

And then Brooke laughed so hard, laughed so hard she pooed herself as well.

And then Ariana, who never wants to be left out, did this poo as well.

Only a baby poo but –

And we were all laughing so hard and, like, shrieking and screaming that Brooke's nanny rushed in and thought one of us had drowned.

And the look on her face!

And because of the scared look on her face, that made us laugh even harder!

And we're sat in André's and we're not really eating a cake and I want to say to them 'Hey Brooke, Ariana and Amber, remember that time in the bath?'

Remember when we were in the bath and we all pooed ourselves and all, like, nearly died laughing?

And then I want them all to say to me, 'Ohmygod, you're crazy!'

'You're really crazy!'

But I sit there and I look at them.

At these girls – these girls who don't really look like girls any more and.

And I know that I won't.

Know that I never would.

Beat.

And then I check my phone and fifty-nine people have hearted Suki Newhouse's warthog picture.

And as I'm looking at it, it suddenly gets another heart.

Another heart –

From Brooke.

c.   And then you're in your room.

You're finally in your room.

And the room's a bit different and Ali must have been here.

And once again, you wonder.

You wonder what he does.

Wonder where he goes.

But then it doesn't really matter because – because *Hiro's Kingdom 5*!

And you quickly change out of school clothes.

And you've made your pillow and bedsheets into a kind of nest.

And then you sit there.

Sit there, waiting.

And then –

And then you begin.

a.   Leonora-Rose Sanford.

As we leave André's, there's Leonora-Rose Sanford.

Coming through the door.

She's with Elena Carvelo and Aisha Premji and this blond guy who looks just like this model we all follow on Instagram because, duh, he is this model we all follow on Instagram.

And as she enters André's, Leonora-Rose's hair kind of bounces.

It literally bounces!

And with that, we all shrink back and push Brooke forward.

The strongest warrior of the pack.

And her and Brooke do this kind of double-kiss thing, this stupid double-kiss thing we all do.

Only there's actually no contact, their faces don't actually touch so it just looks like they are sort of double-checking.

Like maybe there's someone more interesting behind each other's head.

And Brooke's saying, 'God, I love your hair, Leonora-Rose.'

But kind of like she wants to eat it.

And Leonora-Rose's saying 'God, Brooke, you're sweet.'

But kind of like she isn't.

And then Leonora-Rose Sanford and Brooke.

Leonora-Rose and Brooke, who used to be best friends, until last summer when Brooke went to this summer camp that was actually a psychiatric facility –

Leonora-Rose Sanford and Brooke stand there in the doorway of André's, not knowing what to say.

And Brooke's looking at Leonora-Rose.

And Leonora-Rose is looking at Brooke.

And the model from Instagram is looking at his reflection on the camera on his phone.

And because of the silence, to fill the horrible silence, then Brooke panics.

She kind of panics and asks Leonora-Rose about the chemistry test on Monday.

And for a moment, there's a flicker.

A flicker of astonishment that Brooke would mention something so minor, so *entirely nothing* as a school test in front of Leonora-Rose and the blond-haired model from Instagram in the doorway of André's.

A brief flicker before Leonora-Rose recovers.

Before Leonora-Rose laughs.

Says to Brooke, 'Oh, sweetie,' and laughs in Brooke's face.

And Elena Carvelo and Aisha Premji and the blond-haired model from Instagram laugh too.

Laugh like Brooke's a small child.

A toddler who's just wet her knickers.

And Brooke's face behind the oversized Gucci aviators goes this burning crimson red.

And we don't say anything to Brooke, we know not to say anything to Brooke.

But I secretly reach out and touch Brooke's arm.

I secretly reach out and touch Brooke's arm but the acknowledging it is just makes it worse.

And Brooke suddenly springs round and is like:

all.   'Get off me, you fucking fucktard.'

a.   And at this, Leonora Rose raises a perfectly sculpted eyebrow.

Raises a perfectly sculpted eyebrow and laughs.

And Elena Carvelo and Aisha Premji and the blond-haired model from Instagram all laugh too.

And Brooke, Ariana, Amber and me –

Brooke, Ariana, Amber and me, we all just stand there.

Stand there looking at the floor.

And suddenly we're all aware of exactly who we are.

Exactly what we are.

That we're not some sassy pack of fashionistas.

We're not Taylor Swift and Gigi Hadid and Karlie Kloss at the beach for Thanksgiving.

We're not even cool.

And we never will be.

We're just four basic try-hards at the very bottom of the food chain.

And we're nothing.

We're just nothing.

And then Leonora-Rose's saying 'See you at the party, kids,' blowing us a kiss and heading into André's.

But before she does, before she quite reaches the door, she turns around.

Turns and looks at me.

Leonora-Rose.

Leonora-Rose Sanford who has never even said my name.

Turns to me and says 'By the way, I really love what you've done with your lips' and smiles this smile.

And the way, Leonora-Rose smiles –

The way, Leonora-Rose smiles –

Pause.

c. You're in this dark forest.

This dark forest with these mad purple trees.

And the trees' branches are not really branches, they're more like glowing electric veins reaching out to zap you.

And you've found the first enchanted key and now you're heading to the mountain.

And suddenly there's a crash, a massive crash in front of you.

A meteor!

And then another.

And then another.

Huge rocks raining down from the sky.

Skimming just past you.

And you run.

You run and you dodge as the meteors crash around you and the branches of the tree try to grab you.

And you're dodging the meteors and you're moving through the meteor storm.

And the meteors skim past you but they never hit you and you wonder 'Why don't they ever hit you?'

Why don't the meteors ever crush you?

And why aren't the electric trees electrocuting you?

And you're heading to the mountain.

You've got to head to the mountain to save the princess and you need to focus and the meteors are rushing around you and –

And what does someone do, what does someone do to be thrown off a roof?

And – and something about the blue scarf. The boy called Zia and the blue scarf that's not a scarf.

And you're moving through the meteors.

Dodging the meteors.

And you don't want to think about it.

You shouldn't have to think about it.

Just head through the storm.

a.   They're all there when I arrive home.

All standing in the hallway.

Waiting. Smiling.

And as I come in, they all start singing 'Happy Birthday'.

And they're holding balloons and at the end of it, they let go of the balloons.

And the balloons all float to the vaulted ceiling.

And it's nice.

It feels quite nice.

Even though it's just the maids and the housekeeper.

Even though my parents have paid them to do this, it's nice.

It feels quite nice.

And then one of them says a thing, a thing I don't understand.

And all the others laugh.

And then I think how maybe it's not so nice, maybe the moment's not so nice at all.

And then I go to my room.

And the room is big and too cold from the air-conditioning.

And I think about FaceTiming my mother but it's now the middle of the night in Berlin.

And I think about trying my father but it's now the middle of the night in Kiev.

And I look at the number of likes and – one hundred and three people have hearted Suki Newhouse's picture.

And that's when I get the message.

The message from Amber:

'There's no space for you in the car tonight.

Sorry, sweetie.'

Three blown kisses, two shrugging girls, one kiss.

c.   You're on a frozen lake.

You've moved through the enchanted forest and now you're on a frozen lake.

And you're looking for the second key.

And suddenly this creature, this creature's coming towards you: an ice-wolf.

And you run towards the ice-wolf and you stab it with the ice pick you found in the forest.

And the ice-wolf instantly shatters into a thousand pieces.

And then another one rushes at you.

And then another.

And you've got your ice pick and you're stabbing at the ice-wolves and –

And it's easy.

It's so easy.

And you're moving through the frozen tundra and you're killing the ice-wolves.

And snow is falling.

And, and the sky is this blue, this brilliant blue.

And the blue scarf.

Something about the blue scarf.

And you're killing the ice-wolves but then the blue scarf.

The blue scarf.

And why is this so easy?

a.   And I'm sat there in my room.

I'm sitting there in my large, quiet room and I'm scrolling through my phone.

Scrolling through the feed on my phone.

And I can't find what I'm looking for because – because I don't know what I'm looking for.

And then, and then I'm looking in the mirror at the mark above my lip.

At the skin tag that's not even a skin tag.

And I'm remembering this quote.

This quote Elena Carvelo posted on her feed.

That 'Every act of creation is first an act of destruction.'

And I can't remember who said it.

Can't quite remember if Pablo Picasso said it.

Pablo Picasso or maybe Khloé Kardashian and I'm trying to remember.

Trying to think.

And that's when something clicks.

And I run downstairs.

Run downstairs to the kitchens and find it.

Find the thing I've been looking for.

A tiny silver knife the chef uses to gut bluefin tuna.

c.   And then you're no longer on the frozen tundra.

You're up.

You're in your room and you're up.

And you're going through your room.

And you're piling through your room.

Through clothes and comics, shoes and toys.

Lifting up mattresses, emptying drawers.

Hunting as fast as you can.

Looking for the thing you need to find.

Pulling things apart.

Looking. Searching

Because you need to find it.

You really need to find it.

And if you find it, then everything is –

And you just need to find it.

And if you can just find it.

And you're looking, you're looking everywhere.

But it's not here.

And you can't –

You can't –

a.   And then I'm back in my room.

And I know it's time. Know I have to do it.

And I get my phone out. I get my phone out and I pause for a moment.

Find the camera on my phone, switch it to video and find the best angle.

Wedge it on the bookshelf.

And I stand in the centre of the room.

And I hold the knife.

all.   (*Cough*.) Hello everyone at Orchard Hills All-Girls Academy for Academic Excellence. Thank you for watching.

This is for you.

a.   And I pause.

And I take the knife and I hold it against my face.

And –

And I'm just about to begin when I have this idea.

I have this idea in my head that maybe there's something else.

Maybe there's something – bigger.

c.   And you're in your room and you can't find the thing.

Can't find the thing you need to find.

And then you're back on your phone.

You don't want to be but you're back on your phone.

You're looking at your phone. At the video of the man.

The boy on top of the roof.

Zia, pushed off the top of the roof.

And you're looking at the blue scarf he's wearing.

The blue scarf that's a blindfold and – and you don't want to see it.

But you can't help but see it.

The thing that you can't find.

The thing that you've been looking for.

In your room.

The blue scarf.

The blue scarf that is not a blue scarf.

The blue scarf that is actually green.

A green scarf that your sisters gave you on your twelfth birthday.

The same scarf tied tightly around Zia's eyes.

And the man tying it.

The man tying it…

b.   And it's game over.

The game's over and we've stopped playing.

And now we're just standing there.

Standing there exhausted and catching our breath.

And me and Fat Jess are stood there and now no one knows what to say.

And suddenly she blurts out 'I am glad you're not dead!'

I am glad you're not dead!

And then Fat Jess who is not particularly fat at all goes all red.

This, like, really deep red of – well, something really red.

And fair enough, it is quite a dickhead thing to say.

Because.

Wasn't like God was like 'And now I need a volunteer from the Benson family to be accidentally blown up by an undiscovered IED' and my dickhead brother was like 'Yeah alright, I'll do it.'

Wasn't like that at all.

Or – not really.

And yeah, it's a dickhead thing to say, 'I am glad you're not dead', but it's also quite –

It's also quite –

It's also quite –

And I look down and suddenly my hands are wet. There's drops of wetness falling on them.

And what is happening – what the fuck is happening?

This isn't supposed to happen.

I'm not crying!

I'm not crying!

I'm not crying my stupid fucking brains out!

And Fat Jess isn't reaching out. Fat Jess isn't reaching out.

Kind of pulling me towards her.

Holding me.

And I don't need to be held.

I really don't need to be held.

I really –

Pause.

And then – and then I try to wipe my face but my face is covered in this kind of gunk.

And this great big rope of snot has formed a loop from my face to my hand.

And because this great big loop of snot is basically gross, is basically the grossest thing you've ever seen, then Fat Jess kind of laughs.

And I laugh too.

And we're laughing.

We're, like, really laughing.

And I wipe my face.

I dry my eyes and I wipe the snot from my face.

And as I wipe the snot from my face, I notice that Fat Jess –

That *Jess* has eyes the exact same colour as the moss on a rock.

c.   It's green.

The blue scarf is green.

The blue scarf is a green scarf and the green scarf is your scarf.

And you're looking at the video on your phone.

At one of the men.

And the blue scarf that's a green scarf and.

And.

And you're looking at one of the men holding Zia.

One of the official men holding Zia, then pushing him into the air.

Pushing him out into solid air.

Pushing Zia to his death.

And Zia is not a man. He's a boy.

And the man pushing him is not a man either, he's a boy.

The man pushing him is not a man, he's a boy.

The man pushing him is not a man, he's – Ali.

Your sixteen-year-old brother.

Ali.

a.   I can tell they're surprised.

Surprised to see me.

Can tell they're all a little shocked to see me when I arrive at Lily Kwok's Funky Fourteenth Birthday Dance.

I'm wearing my crêpe de Chine blouse with pussybow detailing and I've done my winter metallic contouring.

And I've got the tiny silver knife concealed under my left shoe and my iPhone halfway up my vagina, because Lily's got this photographer from Italian *Vogue* to take the official pictures and everyone has to hand their phone in at the entrance.

And the party's in this French-château-style building that I don't think actually existed two weeks ago.

And when I get there everyone's standing around the edge of this huge dance floor, this huge dance floor in polished-oak parquet that spells out Lily's name.

And everyone –

Everyone in my year at the Orchard Hills All-Girls Academy for Academic Excellence.

Everyone's just standing round the dancefloor, pretending to be twenty years older than they actually are.

Which means they're not really having fun.

And no one's dancing because no one ever dances.

No one could ever dance at Lily Kwok's Funky Fourteenth Birthday Dance.

And suddenly Annika Albrecht sees me and tells Suki Newhouse who then tells Habiba Jallaf.

And a stream of whispers ripples round the room.

And Brooke and Ariana and Amber are in one corner, all dressed in crêpe de Chine blouses with pussybow detailing and all drinking Gold-Leaf Lime Flirtinis with a Himalayan-salt rim.

And I'm standing right beside them by the time they all see me.

And Amber sort of yelps, and Brooke looks sort of petrified and Ariana says nothing, she always says nothing.

And I take my phone out of my vagina and I hand it to Brooke.

Tell her to press 'record' when I give her a signal.

And Brooke looks kind of confused and scared but nods kind of meekly.

And then I go to the DJ and ask him to play this song – this song I say is Lily's favourite.

And then I head into the centre of the dance floor.

The huge empty dance floor with Lily Kwok's name on.

b.   Jess and me, we talk.

We sit there for hours and we just – talk.

We talk about how my mum just sits there all day watching telly.

Watching those channels where they make these crappy birthday cards, then try to sell you all the fiddly shit to make them with.

We talk about how my auntie's always popping in and, like, loving the drama.

Always trying to get my mum to go to Zumba with her.

Even though my mum is like 'Yes, because that's what I really need right now.'

How I'm sort of –

Sort of invisible to them.

We talk about my brother Aron and how weird it is he's dead.

Weird he's dead and how yeah he's a total hero obvs but then how he didn't really have much choice.

How he didn't really like it, the army.

Didn't even really like the sound of fireworks, to be honest.

How he was actually quite – gentle and – nice.

But how there wasn't really anything else for him to do.

And I'm telling Fat Jess how there's an expectation.

A definite expectation.

How everyone sort of thinks that's what I'm gonna do too.

Join up.

Just join up like Aron.

How sort of like that's my only option.

How that's my only option but how actually I've always loved trains.

Although thought they're kind of brilliant.

The way they sort of glide and.

Actually thought I'd like to drive one.

And Jess's all like, 'You could, you totally could.

You could do a course or – go to college or.'

And I'm like 'Nah.'

But then the way she's looking at me?

The way she's looking at me?

c.   And you've got your sword and you're Hiro.

And you're in the Cave of Midnight.

And you're moving through this huge cave.

And you've got your shield and you've got your sword and suddenly an undead cave ghost is coming towards you.

And you knock it back, you knock it back with your shield.

And it just – it just dissolves.

And it's easy.

It's so easy!

And another one comes towards you and you just – push through it.

And – it's not like that.

It's really not like that!

And you're running through the cave and there's this great pit of spikes and you grab the rope and swing over the spikes and – why is it so easy?

Why's it all so easy?

And it's not like that!

Nothing's like that.

And you – you barely know him.

You don't really know him.

You didn't really know him.

And it's not your problem.

It's really not your problem.

And you've got your sword.

You've got your shield and you've got your sword.

And you're Hiro.

You're the hero.

During this next section, as it builds, then the three of them are increasingly drawn into each other's stories, so perhaps a.*'s actions are at times copied by* b. *and* c. *They work together to tell the stories and the distinction between particular moments becomes blurred.*

a.   And I move to the centre of the room, to the centre of the dance floor.

And then I take the lipstick, the Mac Sheen Supreme in the colour 'Native Power' and I trace it perfectly across my lips.

Perhaps they all do this.

I trace it perfectly across my lips and then I take the palm of my hand.

Smear it across my face.

And then I slick two heavy lines of it under my eyes, across my cheeks.

And suddenly everything's stopped.

All the talking has stopped.

b.   And then we talk. Me and Jess just talk.

We sit there on this nothing patch of grass in this nothing town and we just talk.

And I'm saying all this stuff.

All this stuff I've never said.

We're talking about how rubbish this town is.

How we never thought we could leave it.

But how maybe we could leave it together.

She'll be a vet and I'll be a train driver and.

And we'll leave together.

a. And I take the knife.

I take out the knife.

And someone somewhere gasps.

Everyone's standing round the edge of the dance floor.

Watching in silence.

Watching what I'll do next.

And I take the knife and I hold it against my face.

Hold it against the small blemish that is not even a skin tag and definitely not a wart.

And I hold it there.

Hold it there and count to five.

And then I move it down.

Move the knife down to my crêpe de Chine blouse with pussybow detailing.

And that's when I cut.

Cut through the crepe de chine blouse with pussybow detailing until there's a large tear in the fabric.

And then I make another tear.

And then another.

And another.

c. And you're playing your game.

And you're the hero.

You've got your shield and your sword and you're the hero.

And the city's cleaner, the city's cleaner now and life is better.

Life is good.

That's what your brother says, life is good.

And you're just fourteen.

You're just fourteen and it's not your problem.

Just keep moving.

Keep moving through the game.

a.   And then I nod to the DJ.

And I'm shaking, my whole body is shaking.

And the song starts, it starts quite softly.

A beat starts. It doesn't necessarily need to be a song but a pulse or beat that slowly builds.

It's this song I know well, know it off by heart. But right now, it sounds different. Unfamiliar.

And suddenly I'm not sure. For a moment I'm a bit scared.

Something in the beat that's – outside of me.

And I can feel five hundred eyes all on me and it all feels just stupid, really stupid.

And I close my eyes. I have to close my eyes.

And then I make myself move, start to move.

It's barely even movement.

Just this small kind of sway.

b.   We're talking and then we're not-talking.

Suddenly we're not-talking and it's different.

Suddenly the not-talking's different.

a.   And I feel so stupid, just really stupid.

Know that everyone's watching me.

But I just keep going, know I have to keep going.

Just push through it.

b.   And suddenly we're not-talking and I'm looking into her eyes.

Her eyes the exact colour of moss on a rock.

a.   And then the song's building, the song's beginning to build and the words have come in.

And this new thing comes in.

This new sound or.

And something's beginning to change.

b.   And I'm looking into her eyes.

I'm looking into her eyes in the twilight and they're kind of lit up.

Lit up like this night-time animal.

a.   And I can feel my body start to relax, my bones begin to loosen.

And my body begins to move, like really move itself.

And I'm not just swaying any more, I'm beginning to feel it.

To vibrate.

b.   And I look at her and she's looking at me and suddenly it's just – *Oh, fuck*.

There's this, this *rush* of –

a.   And I'm doing this dance, this dance which is not really dancing.

It's not really dancing but it's something else.

b.   This rush that makes me weak at the knees.

It really does!

Because she is beautiful, she is actually really beautiful.

She's the most beautiful girl in this town.

Possibly the universe.

a. And the song's building and this song's building.

  And it's stupid and it's crap but it also feels good.

b. She is Rihanna, Lauren Cockcroft from Year 11, and all
  my favourite video girls made into one perfect being and
  why have I never see this?

  Why did I not see this before?

a. And the words are still words but they're sort of drifting
  out and becoming something else.

  Something new.

c. And you're in the cave.

  You're in the Cave of Midnight and you're killing the
  cave ghosts.

a. And I'm beginning to feel the sound.

  Begin to feel it take over.

c. And you've got your shield and you've got your sword
  and the cave ghosts are just falling around you.

  And you keep moving forward and, and –

  And it's not like that.

  The world's not like that.

  It's not like that.

  It's really not like that.

  People die and, and people kill each other.

  And they don't just –

  And, and –

b. And why did I not see this before?

  Why did I not see this before?

c. And, and you don't care if the city's cleaner!

  And you don't care if life is good now!

And you don't care if they found Zia with another lad!

And you don't care what he was doing with another lad and you don't think it's a sin punishable with death!

And you don't think it's a reason to push people off rooftops and you don't believe it is the Almighty's will!

And this is not a game, this is not a video game, it's real life and real death.

And what kind of world do we live in where sixteen-year-old boys throw terrified teenage boys who like skateboarding and Drake off rooftops to their deaths?

And what kind of world do we live in where a crowd of adults gathers below to watch adult men throw teenage boys who like skateboarding and Drake to their deaths?

And what kind of world do we live in where a man and woman let their sixteen-year-old son throw teenage boys who like skateboarding and Drake to their deaths and do nothing, they do nothing.

And what kind of world do we live in where adults convince teenage boys to throw other teenage boys to their deaths in the name of the Almighty?

And what can anyone do with their body, what can you anyone do with their body and someone else's body that could ever deserve that?

And where are the grown-ups to do something, where are the grown-ups in this story and

and who can do something to change this world?

Who is doing something to change this world?

And you're sat there playing your game.

You're just sat there playing your game when you –

When *I* –

When I realise that the person to do something is *me*.

It's me.

a.   And I'm beginning to feel the sound.

I'm beginning to move with the sound.

And my eyes are still shut.

My eyes are shut tight.

And I don't think I can open them.

b.   And, and I want to kiss her, I really do.

But I don't think I can move.

There's approximately twenty-five centimetres between her mouth and mine but I don't think I can move.

a.   And I want to open my eyes but I don't think I can.

I can feel the room on me and I don't think I can.

And then, and then the sound changes.

The sound changes and something shifts.

b.   And I don't think I can kiss her but then something changes, something shifts.

And then I do.

I move forward and she moves forward and I'm kissing her!

I'm actually kissing her!

a.   And I open my eyes.

I open my eyes and everyone's looking at me.

Five hundred fearful eyes all on me.

And I'm not afraid.

I'm really not afraid!

b.   I'm kissing her and it is just – just brilliant!

And I'm not afraid.

I'm not afraid of anything.

a.   And I'm shaking my head.

      I'm shaking my head and I'm pulling at my hair and I'm
      wiggling my arse and I'm grabbing my breasts.

b.   It's like nothing I have ever felt before.

      Like nothing I can understand.

a.   And I remember this word for them.

      This really weird word for them.

      Dugs.

      That's what they call breasts, what someone somewhere
      calls them.

      Dugs.

      And that's what I've got now.

      Dugs. Dugs, dugs, dugs!

b.   And I realise there's so much more.

      There's so much more than I ever thought there was.

a.   And I'm shaking my dugs.

      I'm shaking my dugs and my hair and my vaj and my feet.

      And I'm making these noises, these wild, howling noises.

      I'm moving like a crazed thing, like a wild feral animal.

b.   And everything's just sliding away.

      In this moment, everything's just sliding away.

a.   And I look up.

      I look straight at Brooke and Amber and Ariana.

      Aisha, Elena, Leonora-Rose.

      I look them in the eyes and all I can see is fear.

      And I want to say them, 'What are you scared of?'

      'What's the thing you're so scared of people seeing?'

'What's the thing inside you you're so ashamed of?'

And I want to take their fear away.

b.   And it's not a feeling.

It's not a feeling, it's a place.

It's an actual place.

a.   I want to take their fear away and replace it with love.

And I have enough love.

I have enough love for them all!

c.   And then I'm growing stronger.

I'm not in a cave or looking for an enchanted key.

I'm on this great plain.

I'm on this great plain and, and I can feel myself getting stronger.

Can feel myself growing in power.

a.   And with every beat, I'm getting stronger.

With every beat, I'm being transformed.

c.   I'm no longer just bones, skin and water.

I'm composed of a new kind of material.

b.   And all that exists, all that exists is this place, this one golden place we've been looking for.

And everything else is just fading away.

a.   And it's wide open. And I can see everything.

I can see it all.

b.   This place that we've been looking for.

a.   And in this place there's no grown-ups and there's nothing broken.

c.   And I'm on this great plain.

And, and it's not a game.

It's a new place I've never been to.

b.   And there's no time, there's no bodies.

There's no me, there's no Jess.

c.   There's no school, there's no boredom, there's no stress, there's no fear.

b.   There's no orders of service, no bunches of cheap flowers, no howls in the middle of the night.

c.   No more families disappearing in the middle of the night.

No more sixteen-year-olds pushed to their deaths.

a.   No more feeling ugly and useless because you're not a Kardashian.

No starving yourself till your ribs stick out like a bony dog.

b.   No broken glass, no square root of fuck-knows-what, no brown envelopes collecting by the door.

c.   No more good sides and bad sides, no more killing in the name of a peaceful god, no more making up history.

a.   No more trying to be more grown-up when all the grown-ups around you are really lost, no more magazines telling you how to breathe.

c.   No more thinking someone is wrong because they don't look and think exactly like you do.

b.   No streets of empty shops, no dead-end factory jobs, no fake-tit fantasies.

a.   No more adults blaming us for everything they've created.

b.   No more blaming us for everything you've created.

c.   No more blaming us for everything we've inherited.

a.   No more thinking that nothing can ever change, no more thinking that nothing will ever change.

c.   No more accepting this sad, broken world we've been given.

a.   And I feel this connection, this connection to something else.

c.   A faint silver line connecting me to something else.

a.   Like I'm part of some ancient tribe, a new but ancient tribe.

Like I'm part of something bigger.

c.   A new tribe, a new tribe that is coming.

b.   And I feel this connection.

Like I'm not alone.

a.   A new tribe that will make things better.

c.   A better world that's coming.

b.   Something new coming.

c.   Something...

The NATIVES *come together. It's incredible.*

b.   And then, and then I feel so joyful, so overwhelmed in this moment that I want to sort of keep it.

To lock it down.

a.   No more feeling ashamed because you are not perfect.

b.   And I get my phone out and I start recording.

a.   No fake kisses that are not really kisses.

b.   And we're kissing and I'm recording and we're kissing and I'm recording.

a.   No more thinking that you are not enough, no more just trying to keep up.

b.   And then to be honest, I'm getting a bit – yeah. A little bit – hard.

a.   No more cool people, no more fucking cool people.

b.   And we're kissing and we're laughing and I'm looking at
      her through the screen.

      a. *stops what she's doing.*

      And then I get this idea. I'm getting this idea.

      Because I want her to see it. I just need Jess to – see it.
      Just for a moment.

      And the idea just – it won't go away. It's just something
      I need to –

      And I'm holding the phone with one hand and with the
      other hand I sort of, sort of –

      Take it out.

      And, she's a little bit surprised. I think she's definitely
      a little bit shocked. But she's still trying to keep the
      moment. She's trying to be cool.

      And she says my name – not in a horrible way, more like
      [*'What you doing?'*] 'Come on, mate.'

      But I'm touching it now. I'm really touching it now and –
      it's like the train has left the station and I've gone too far.

      And something else is taking over.

      And I'm looking at it all through the little window on my
      phone and it's hot, it's really hot.

      Which makes me touch it even more.

      And I'm touching it and I'm looking at her and I'm
      touching it and – and she doesn't really move.

      And I hear myself saying all this stuff.

      Stuff I've never said before but the stuff they always say.

      All the stuff they say.

      And I'm looking down at her but it's not really.

      Not really *Jess* any more.

      I mean it is her but on the screen it's.

I dunno.

And I'm going for it now. And it's so hot. It's so fucking hot.

And I'm really going for it now. I'm standing over it, standing over her, filming it and I'm going for it.

And she's kind of looking at me and the sad look on her face tells me this is nothing new.

Tells me she's been here before.

I'm gonna shoot on your face, I say. I'm gonna fucking shoot it all over your fucking face, I say.

And she just sits there, why does she just sit there?

And then I say it and then I do it. That's what I do. I shoot it. All on her face. All over her face. And it's sort of like it is. Sort of like it is in the – but then really not.

And I touch her face.

I bring my hand up to her face. I touch her face and there's this, like, globby mess all over her and I scoop it up.

I scoop it up and it's like, just for a second, just for a second, she thinks, she thinks this is something else.

An act of tenderness or.

And then with my other hand, I sort of ease her mouth open. I sort of ease her mouth open and. Feed it to her.

Because that's how it ends. That's my favourite ending.

And there's this look that – I mean, I have never seen this look. And it's crazy, it's so completely crazy that I've done this and that look and everything that it makes me want to laugh, y'know?

So I do.

a.   And I'm dancing and then I'm not dancing. And then the song stops and I'm just standing there.

Standing there in the centre of the dance floor.

b. I laugh.

I stand there looking down into her face with this globby, gobby mess and I laugh.

a. And I'm standing in the centre of the dance floor.

And nobody claps or cheers or – anything.

Nobody dares move.

And everyone's quiet.

Everything's quiet.

Quiet apart from the small, dry sobs coming from the direction of Lily Kwok.

b. And I don't remember how Jess leaves but obviously she does.

Once she's.

Leaves quite quickly actually.

And there's part of me that's still – there's part of me that's going 'It's okay. It's fine. No biggie, you know?'

Like, maybe it wasn't ideal or.

But it's all okay.

It's all good.

c. And I'm on my phone, looking at the screen.

And I'm looking at the video.

The video of Zia falling from the sky.

And I'm editing the images and I'm making my own film, my own film all about Zia.

And I go to Zia's profile and I find all these pictures of Zia and I make a film.

And there's Zia as a very fat baby sitting on his grandmother's knee.

There's five-year-old Zia grinning in the bath.

Zia on a fairground ride, terrified but thrilled.

Zia dancing with friends.

Zia smoking a cigarette and trying to be cool.

Zia on his skateboard.

And then the clip. The clip of Zia falling through the air.

And I make this film, I find all these pictures of Zia and the video of Zia falling and I make this film.

And then I put some words at the end.

Some words in my very bad English.

all.   This is Zia, I write.

He was killed by a boy called Ali Soomekh, I write.

Zia was sixteen years old, I write.

He did not deserve this.

Please *someone do something*, I write.

b.   And then I make myself another toastie.

Go on *Hiro's Kingdom 5* for a bit. Just to chill out. Calm down.

And then I think maybe I'll send her a text. Just to say hi or.

c.   Please *someone do something*, I write.

b.   Yo, I say.

That was a bit mad, I say.

Wasn't it, I say.

Say something, I say.

Please just say something, I say.

And then, finally: a bleep from my pocket.

Jess.

'I feel very sad for you,' she says.

c.   Please *someone do something*, I write.

b.   'I feel very sad for boys like you,' she says.

      'I really wish your brother was still around for you,' she
      says.

      'See ya,' she says.

      No smiley faces, no sad faces.

      No – [*Nothing.*]

a.   I'm standing there in the centre of the room.

      Standing in the centre of the dance floor.

      Standing there, just breathing.

      And everyone's looking at me, everyone at the party's
      looking at me.

      Waiting for my next move.

b.   And I feel just –

      I feel –

a.   And I slowly walk back to Brooke.

      Brooke who's holding my phone, who's filmed everything
      on my phone.

      And as I walk back to Brooke, everyone sort of moves
      aside.

      Moves aside like, like I'm strapped with explosives.

      And I take the phone off Brooke and as I do so, she gives
      me this look.

      This look I've never seen before.

      Maybe fear or –

      Or something –

      And I realise that it's not enough.

      I realise that tonight is not enough.

And I take the phone off Brooke.

I take the phone off Brooke and everyone at Lily Kwok's Funky Fourteenth is still silent.

And I find the film on my phone.

And I think about what would happen – what would happen if everyone saw it.

If my parents –

If my teachers –

If the Massachusetts Institute of Technology –

If the entire island –

If everyone I will one day know but haven't yet met –

If everyone in my present and everyone in my future, everyone in the whole world saw this film.

Saw me for who I am.

And the idea is –

And the idea is –

b.   And I get this idea.

And then I'm on this site.

This site where you can upload – just whatever.

And I've got the film of me and Jess and –

Because – because I've sent Jess fifteen texts.

Because I've sort of said I'm sorry.

Because today is my birthday, my fourteenth birthday, and, I mean, fuck her – fuck that fucking bitch.

And something in me, something in me is taking over and –

And I'm gonna do it.

I need to do it.

Because I hate myself so much right now that I need to do it.

Because it's so easy and why is it so easy?

And what has happened to my brain?

What is happening in my brain?

And why is so it easy?

Why is everything so easy?

Who made it so easy?

And I'm going to do it.

I have to do it.

a.   And I think can I do it?

Can I really do it?

And I'm thinking about the way that everyone cleared a path around me as I left the dance floor.

And suddenly I realise that's what it is.

That's what the film is.

A bomb.

A bomb in a small tunnel.

Destroying the path behind me.

c.   And I think can I do it?

Can I really do it?

And I think about my parents.

And I think my brother.

And what will happen.

And I don't know what will happen.

And – and why should I do something.

Why should it be me to do something?

b.   And I'm gonna do it.

I'm really gonna do it.

Because I have no choice.

Because it's so easy.

Because I'm sick.

I'm sick and I'm filthy and I have no choice.

c.   And why should it be me to do something?

Because I'm not a man.

I'm just a fourteen-year-old boy.

I'm just this fourteen-year-old boy.

And why isn't someone doing something?

Where are the adults to do something?

Where are the heroes?

And is this what it feels like to be the hero?

Does it feel just like fear?

a.   And I want to go further.

To see what happens next.

To see what happens when I burn things down.

b.   And I type in a title.

a.   I'm on this website and I type in the title.

c.   I finish editing the film and I type in a title.

a.   'Watch Me Dance Like I've Never Danced Before.'

b.   'Watch This Little Slut Get A Creamy Faceful, Lol.'

c.   'This is a boy called Zia. Please watch.'

a.   And I'm looking at the screen.

b.   I'm looking at the screen and it's asking me if I want to post.

c.   I'm looking at the screen and my finger's over the screen.

a.   My finger's over the screen and –

b.   And there's a space.

a.   There's a distance.

c.   There's the tiniest distance.

a.   The distance between my finger and the screen.

b.   The smallest distance.

c.   The distance of nothing.

a.   The distance between your eyeball and your brain.

b.   And I'm gonna do it.

       I'm thinking how much I hate my life and I'm gonna do it.

a.   And I thinking what will happen next.

       Of where it will go.

       Of all the places it will go.

c.   And I'm thinking what happens next.

       I'm thinking about Zia and my brother and my family and –

b.   And I'm going to do it.

       Because I hate Jess so much right now.

       Because I hate myself so much right now I'm really going
       to do it.

a.   And I'm thinking where it will go.

       How it will start here and then go outwards.

       Beyond this island.

       Beyond all limits.

       Beyond all boundaries.

b.   And then I'm thinking about my brother Aron.

       I'm thinking about Aron in the box and Aron not in the box.

And then I'm thinking about Jess.

I'm thinking about the way she looked at me, the way she looked at me before.

And I'm thinking how maybe there's something new.

Maybe I don't have to be this thing I am.

Maybe I can do something new.

Maybe I can be something new.

c.   And I'm thinking about Zia.

I'm thinking about Zia and all the people who will see him.

All the people who will know him.

All the places he will go.

b.   And I feel something bigger.

Bigger than my life.

Bigger than my past.

a.   And I feel this connection.

This connection to a new tribe.

A new but ancient tribe.

A tribe of wild, ragged beasts.

c.   And I'm so scared.

I'm so scared but I think maybe this is the start.

Maybe this is the beginning.

This is how it begins.

b.   And I'm looking at the screen.

a.   I'm looking at the screen and.

c.   I'm looking at the screen and I'm holding it in my hand.

b.   The distance between your eyeball and your brain.

c.   I'm holding it in my hand.

a.   The power's in my hand.

b.   The power's here.

a.   And I'm looking at the screen.

b.   I'm looking at the screen and I know what I'm going to do.

c.   I'm looking at the screen and I know what I have to do.

a.   I'm looking at the screen and it's beginning to change.

b.   Something's beginning to change.

c.   Everything's beginning to change.

a.   The distance between your eyeball and your brain.

b.   There's a new world that is coming that is –

a.   There's a new world that is coming that is –

c.   There's a new world that's coming that is –

      Ends.

A Nick Hern Book

Natives first published in Great Britain as a paperback original in 2017 by Nick Hern Books Limited, The Glasshouse, 49a Goldhawk Road, London W12 8QP, in association with Boundless Theatre

Natives copyright © 2017 Glenn Waldron

Glenn Waldron has asserted his right to be identified as the author of this work

Cover image: photography by Lidia Crisafulli; artwork by Spy

Designed and typeset by Nick Hern Books, London
Printed in the UK by Mimeo Ltd, Huntingdon, Cambridgeshire PE29 6XX

A CIP catalogue record for this book is available from the British Library

ISBN 978 1 84842 639 9

www.nickhernbooks.co.uk

facebook.com/nickhernbooks

twitter.com/nickhernbooks